USING POPULAR LITERATURE

To Teach Reading and Writing Skills

Shane • Sounder • The Old Man and the Sea
The Call of the Wild • The Red Pony

Book 1

COPYRIGHT © 1993 Mark Twain Media, Inc.

Printing No. CD-1852

Mark Twain Media, Inc. Publishers
Distributed by Carson-Dellosa Publishing Company, Inc.

♦ CONTENTS ♦

♦ INTRODUCTION ♦

Teaching a short novel to a class of students with widely divergent skills, abilities, and motivations can be challenging. This activity book is designed to provide for all levels of learning in your class through the use of popular short novels.

Several activities are designed to teach basic reading skills on the basis of reading the synopsis alone. The **Word Study** provides vocabulary work which will make the synopsis more understandable, and the **Anticipation Guide** will peak the students' interest in what is to come while allowing them the opportunity to project and imagine themselves in situations similar to those in the novel. The **Word Search** puzzle incorporates all of the vocabulary from the Word Study, as well as some pertinent facts given in the synopsis. The **Author Profile** can be completed using the biographical sketch provided and other resources from the library.

The **Questions for Study and Discussion** are separated into literal, interpretive, and critical levels and may be used with students who are reading the entire novel. While the **Activities** page suggests enrichment activities, the **Vocabulary** includes words, in context, that will contribute to easier reading and understanding of the novel. The **Crossword** puzzle incorporates all of the vocabulary words as a means of reinforcement. A **Test** is included which covers the entire novel.

Of the Supplemental Activities, **In My Opinion . . .** provides students with an opportunity for self-expressive writing. The **Plot Graph** can be used as a visual aid in demonstrating how an author weaves and develops a plot. This activity may be used individually, or the graph can be enlarged and used by the entire class. Students' opinions may vary as to what, for them, are the most significant events in the novel.

These activities can be used as either a brief, overall view of a short novel, or as an in-depth teaching guide. However used, they will serve to reinforce reading and writing skills for students at all learning levels while introducing young people to some of the most popular short novels.

Date _____ Name_____

SHORT NOVEL ASSIGNMENT CHECKLIST

Title: _____

Assignment	Date Assigned	Date Due
Synopsis	_____	_____
Biography/Author Profile	_____	_____
Word Study	_____	_____
Anticipation Guide	_____	_____
Word Search	_____	_____
Questions for Study and Discussion		
Literal Level	_____	_____
Interpretive Level	_____	_____
Critical Level	_____	_____
Vocabulary	_____	_____
Crossword Puzzle	_____	_____
Student Activity Assignments		
_____	_____	_____
_____	_____	_____
_____	_____	_____
_____	_____	_____

Notes:

SHANE

by Jack Schaefer

SYNOPSIS

Young Bob Starrett watched the man ride into the valley. Not a big man—slender, really, but slender like a steel blade. Graceful, yet with a deadly look about him. He was dressed differently from the men Bob knew, with a kind of elegance that was evident despite the dust from the road. He and his horse were thirsty. That was obvious long before he asked Joe Starrett, Bob's father, if he could use the pump. What fascinated Bob was the way that the stranger carefully washed his face and arms and brushed the dust off his clothes. He even combed his hair. It seemed strange to Bob that somebody would take such care about how he looked out here on the range. Then, as the man started to leave, Bob's father did an unexpected thing. He asked the stranger to stay for dinner and bed down for the night. The man was appreciative, and Bob's father introduced himself and his son. The stranger also introduced himself. "Call me Shane," he said. Shane. It was a name that people around here would not forget for awhile. Not for a long, long while.

The American West, as most people think of it, was and still is a particular geographical region, from the Great Plains to the Pacific Ocean. It is a huge region, covering a broad expanse of land. However, there is another American West. It is not just a geographical region, but a mythical region of legends and epic heroes. And this American West is pretty much as one might expect, with its standard population of cowboys, cattle barons, gunfighters, gamblers, and, in general, a familiar cast of characters to be found in most western stories and dramas. This mythical American West does have a basis in historical reality. The reality, of course, was never as romantic as the myths. Yet, there was a brief period when the real West did come close to being like the Wild West of story and legend.

Historically, the period began shortly after the Civil War and lasted for about two decades, until the 1880's. It was the period of the cattle kingdom, when the Great Plains, from Texas to the Canadian border, were a broad, unfenced sea of grass. Cattle could be branded and left free to graze at will, then rounded up and driven to towns like Abilene and Dodge City, near the southern range, and in the north to towns like Cheyenne, Wyoming, where railroad cars waited to ship the cattle east.

Gamblers, dance hall girls, and plenty of liquor were also waiting in the cowtowns to provide the cowboys with a good time and relieve them of their wages. There were also enough gunfighters around to keep things lively.

The railroads, which helped to make the cattle kingdom possible, also helped to end it by bringing trainloads of homesteaders to the West. Most of the newcomers were farmers.

Under the Homestead Act of 1862, they could, after five years of working the land, get legal title to 160 acres—even if cattlemen considered the land theirs. It wasn't the cattlemen's, really. It was public land, which the government could legally give to homesteaders if it chose to do so. Nevertheless, the cattlemen fought the homesteaders, until eventually there were too many to fight. By 1889, homesteaders were fencing in the range as far west as the Rockies. The days of the cattle kingdom, and all that went with it, were coming to a close.

It is at this time, in Jack Schaefer's novel, that the mysterious Shane comes riding in to one of the high valleys where the Great Plains meet the Rockies. Shane, in many ways, fits the myth of the western hero—good with his fists and with a gun, yet decent and honorable—a man larger than life. At the same time, the author's descriptive detail makes Shane a credible hero–a real person, despite the myth. The heroic mold itself seems plausible, considering that the story is told from the viewpoint of a hero-worshiping boy. Shane's personal story, though never told directly, is clearly that of a man trying to put his past behind him and begin a new and better life—a not uncommon situation in Western fiction.

The situation that the Starretts and other homesteaders face is also standard–the conflict with the big rancher—in this case, Luke Fletcher, who is trying to drive them off the land. Yet these and other elements of the typical Western novel are supported with enough realistic and historically accurate details that stereotyped situations do not seem stereotyped. Even so, as in most Westerns, the heart of the novel is suspense, climaxed by action.

The suspense begins soon after Shane agrees to stay on and work for Joe Starrett. Although Shane has never done farmwork before, he learns quickly and does it well. And unlike most men of his time, he does not seem to consider farmwork beneath him. In fact, he seems to be enjoying himself. Bob notes how he begins to relax after awhile.

But all the while, Fletcher keeps pushing Joe Starrett to sell out, and he pushes hard. Before Shane, Joe had another, younger man working for him, but Fletcher's men roughed up the young man at the saloon in town and scared him off. Hiring another man so soon afterward, which Joe has done, is a challenge to Fletcher. There seems to be little doubt that Fletcher will have his men try to scare Shane away, too.

Shane is hardly someone to be scared off, but he has found peace with himself while working for Starrett, and he would like to keep his fighting days in the past. Yet, even though he doesn't care what anybody thinks of him—even if they think he is a coward—he does care what they think of Joe Starrett. And if he is working for Joe, what he does reflects on Joe. So, he winds up having to fight Fletcher's men. And fight them he does, with some timely help from Joe.

Shane and Joe win the fight with Fletcher's men, but this is not going to end the trouble. If anything, it will goad Fletcher into more desperate measures. If one way won't work, another might.

In the end, of course, neither Fletcher nor the other big cattlemen can win. Too many homesteaders are moving west. But if Fletcher can keep them out of this valley for awhile, he'll be all right. He has a contract from the federal government to supply beef to the Indian agent at a Sioux reservation, and he wants more land on which to run his cattle. There is a lot of money involved. Thus, in the short run, as well as the long run, the fight on both sides is for economic survival. And in this valley, it will be a fight to the finish.

Shane, having sized up the overall situation, wants to stay out of it, personally. Nevertheless, he has made his decision. He will stand with Joe Starrett and the homesteaders, though he doesn't much respect any of them, except Joe. Shane has already guessed what Fletcher will do next, and when he hears that Fletcher has hired a gunfighter named Stark Wilson, he knows he guessed correctly. The idea is to pick on a hothead among the homesteaders—someone who might be fool enough to let himself be pushed into drawing his gun—and make an example of him—an example to frighten the other homesteaders.

Shane is sadly familiar with such tactics, perhaps because in the past he has been involved with them himself, or so the reader might guess. But now—now Shane knows what he will have to do.

Shane's presence has made a difference in the valley, and he will have left something of himself here in the memories of the people whose lives he has affected, especially Bobby. But for Shane himself, for his own life, however the final confrontation with Wilson and Fletcher comes out, he has lost. He has lost the battle to change what he is. But no matter. For the sake of the Starretts, Shane must do what he must do.

What do you think Shane will do? To find out, read the rest of the story!

BIBLIOGRAPHY

Burke, W.J. and Will D. Howe, *American Authors and Books: 1640 to the Present Day*. New York: Crown Publishers, Inc., 1962.

Ethridge, James M. and Barbara Kopala, *Contemporary Authors*, Vols. 11-12, Detroit: Gale Research Company, 1965.

James, Mertice M. and others, *The Book Review Digest*. New York.

JACK SCHAEFER

Born in Cleveland, Ohio, on November 19, 1907, Jack Schaefer earned an A.B. degree from Oberlin College in 1929. After attending Columbia University as a graduate student, he began a career as a reporter for United Press in 1930. Later, he became editor of a New Haven, Connecticut newspaper and an editorial writer for the Baltimore *Sun*. Schaefer began working as a free lance writer in 1949.

Schaefer's novel, *Shane*, was the first novel he published, and some critics believe it is the best western ever written. So it is particularly interesting to note that, prior to writing the novel, Schaefer had never been farther west than Ohio, and he was not an avid reader of western fiction. He chose to write western fiction primarily because of his interest in American history, and research provided him with the background he needed to write serious western literature.

As a journalist, Schaefer preferred writing editorial essays to reporting. He once said, "I'm reasonably certain that if I had done much reporting, I would have ruined myself as a writer." His writing style has been described as "clear, realistic, focused on its subject, and powerfully written." His characters are not stereotypical heroes and villains, but believable individuals who adapt to the challenges of the old West.

In addition to *Shane* (1949), Jack Schaefer wrote a number of novels for children, including *First Blood* (1953), *The Canyon* (1953), *Old Ramon* (1960), *The Plainsmen* (1963), *Stubby Pringle's Christmas* (1964), *New Mexico* (1967) and *Mavericks* (1967). In 1985 he received the Western Writers of America Golden Spur Award for the best western novel ever written for *Shane*. He also wrote a number of westerns and short stories for adults. Gradually, however, Schaefer became dissatisfied with his writing. He was increasingly concerned with human destruction of the natural world and felt that he was contributing to the problem. His writings after 1967 were more about animals and the land.

Jack Schaefer died January 24, 1991, in Santa Fe, New Mexico.

Bibliography
Something About the Author, Vol. 66. New York: Gale Research Co., 1991.

Date _____ Name _____

AUTHOR PROFILE

Some of the answers to the following questions may be found in the biography on the preceding page. For other information, check your library.

AUTHOR'S NAME :   *Jack Schaefer*

1. What has this author written?_____

_____

2. Date of birth _____ Date of death _____

3. What does/did this author look like? _____

_____

_____

4. Where did this author grow up? _____

5. Did this author have any particular difficulties in life? What were they?

_____

_____

6. What kinds of things does/did this author like to write about most? _____

_____

7. What kind of education does/did this author have? _____

8. What kinds of jobs did this author hold? _____

9. What did you find to be particularly interesting when reading about this author's life?

_____

_____

10. If you could talk to this author in person, what would you like to ask him?

_____

Date _____ Name _____

(WORD STUDY)

Define the underlined words:

1. It seemed strange to Bob that somebody would take such care about how he looked out here on the range.

_____

2. This mythical American West does have a basis in historical reality.

_____

3. Cattle could be branded and left free to graze at will . . .

_____

4. Nevertheless, the cattlemen fought the homesteaders, until eventually there were too many to fight.

_____

5. . . . stereotyped situations do not seem stereotyped.

_____

6. Even so, as in most Westerns, the heart of the novel is suspense, climaxed by action.

_____

7. Hiring another man so soon afterward, which Joe has done, is a challenge to Fletcher.

_____

8. Thus, in the short run, as well as the long run, the fight on both sides is for economic survival.

_____

9. The idea is to pick a hothead among the homesteaders . . .

_____

10. But for Shane himself, for his own life, however the final confrontation with Wilson and Fletcher comes out, he has lost.

_____

Date _____ Name _____

ANTICIPATION GUIDE

for the novel *Shane*

The numbered questions can be answered from reading the synopsis for the novel. Express your own thoughts when answering the questions that are marked with a ⇒.

1. What is the name of the young boy in the story? _____

    ⇒How do you think the boy and Shane will get along? _____

_____

2. What kind of a man is Shane?_____

_____

    ⇒What do you think happened in Shane's past that he is trying to forget?

_____

_____

3. What happened to the hired hand that worked for Joe Starrett before Shane came?

_____

_____

    ⇒Do you think the same thing will happen to Shane? Why or why not?

_____

_____

4. Why does Luke Fletcher want to get rid of the homesteaders? _____

_____

    ⇒Do you think all of the homesteaders are the "good guys"? _____

_____

5. Whose side does Shane take in the fight? _____

_____

    ⇒Whom do you think will die in the final confrontation?_____

_____

Date _____ Name _____

SHANE
Word Search

Using the clues below, find the answers hidden in the puzzle and circle them. They may be printed horizontally, vertically, diagonally, or backward. All of the words are associated with the novel in some way.

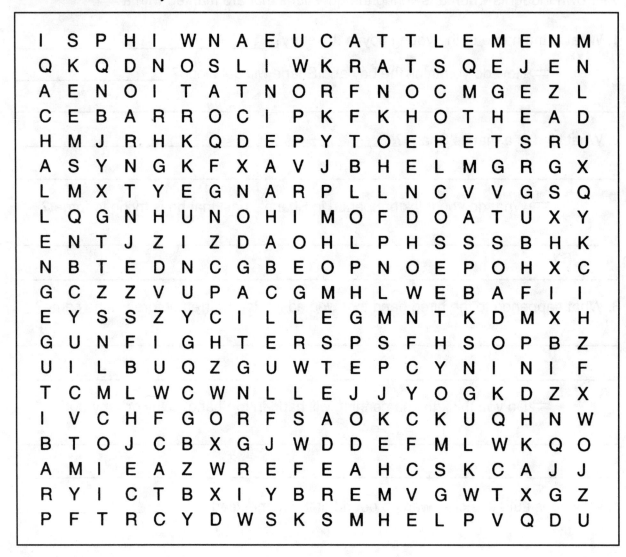

```
I  S  P  H  I  W  N  A  E  U  C  A  T  T  L  E  M  E  N  M
Q  K  Q  D  N  O  S  L  I  W  K  R  A  T  S  Q  E  J  E  N
A  E  N  O  I  T  A  T  N  O  R  F  N  O  C  M  G  E  Z  L
C  E  B  A  R  R  O  C  I  P  K  F  K  H  O  T  H  E  A  D
H  M  J  R  H  K  Q  D  E  P  Y  T  O  E  R  E  T  S  R  U
A  S  Y  N  G  K  F  X  A  V  J  B  H  E  L  M  G  R  G  X
L  M  X  T  Y  E  G  N  A  R  P  L  L  N  C  V  V  G  S  Q
L  Q  G  N  H  U  N  O  H  I  M  O  F  D  O  A  T  U  X  Y
E  N  T  J  Z  I  Z  D  A  O  H  L  P  H  S  S  S  B  H  K
N  B  T  E  D  N  C  G  B  E  O  P  N  O  E  P  O  H  X  C
G  C  Z  Z  V  U  P  A  C  G  M  H  L  W  E  B  A  F  I  I
E  Y  S  S  Z  Y  C  I  L  L  E  G  M  N  T  K  D  M  X  H
G  U  N  F  I  G  H  T  E  R  S  P  S  F  H  S  O  P  B  Z
U  I  L  B  U  Q  Z  G  U  W  T  E  P  C  Y  N  I  N  I  F
T  C  M  L  W  C  W  N  L  L  E  J  J  Y  O  G  K  D  Z  X
I  V  C  H  F  G  O  R  F  S  A  O  K  C  K  U  Q  H  N  W
B  T  O  J  C  B  X  G  J  W  D  D  E  F  M  L  W  K  Q  O
A  M  I  E  A  Z  W  R  E  F  E  A  H  C  S  K  C  A  J  J
R  Y  I  C  T  B  X  I  Y  B  R  E  M  V  G  W  T  X  G  Z
P  F  T  R  C  Y  D  W  S  K  S  M  H  E  L  P  V  Q  D  U
```

1. the first name of the young boy in the novel
2. a defiant, face to face encounter
3. a person who uses guns to fight with
4. author of *Shane* (two words)
5. the gunman who was hired by Luke Fletcher
6. the geographical region where the novel takes place
7. what men who raise cattle are called
8. financial
9. people who accepted U.S. land grants
10. fictional
11. a standard conception of something
12. an invitation to fight, or a dare
13. to nibble on grass in a pasture
14. a quick-tempered person
15. land where cattle are raised
16. a state of uncertainty, excitement

8

Date _____   Name _____

QUESTIONS FOR STUDY AND DISCUSSION

for the novel *Shane*

Literal Level

1. What is the setting of *Shane*—both location and time period?

_____

_____

2. What happened to the hired hand who worked for Joe Starrett before Shane came?

_____

_____

3. What does Shane have hidden in his saddle-roll?

_____

_____

4. Who does Fletcher hire to help him drive the homesteaders away from the valley?

_____

_____

5. What happened to Ernie Wright?

_____

_____

6. After Fletcher tells Joe he will buy his farm—or else—what does Shane do to keep Joe from fighting Fletcher and Wilson?

_____

_____

7. Who is killed in the gunfight?

_____

_____

8. What does Shane do after the fight?

_____

_____

Date _____ Name _____

QUESTIONS FOR STUDY AND DISCUSSION

for the novel *Shane*

Interpretive Level

1. Explain the differences in the ways that Fletcher and Joe Starrett think the land should be used.

_____

_____

_____

2. What does Joe and Shane's struggle with the tree stump symbolize?

_____

_____

_____

3. What evidence is given that Shane was probably a gunfighter in the past?

_____

_____

_____

4. Why does Joe never ask Shane why he keeps a gun hidden in his saddle-roll?

_____

_____

_____

5. Why does Shane walk away when Chris insults him at Grafton's?

_____

_____

_____

Date _____ Name _____

QUESTIONS FOR STUDY AND DISCUSSION

for the novel *Shane*

Critical Level

1. What do you believe is the internal conflict that Shane is trying to deal with?

_____

_____

_____

_____

2. What reason do you think the author might have had for naming his characters Bob, Joe, Shane, and Stark Wilson?

_____

_____

_____

_____

3. What were Joe and Marian Starrett fighting for? Was it worth it?

_____

_____

_____

_____

ACTIVITIES

for the novel *Shane*

♣ Make a bulletin board display using photographs of life in Wyoming during the 1880's. Use these as a basis for discussion about the lifestyles of the homesteaders.

♣ Shane is a mystery when he comes to the valley, and he is still a mystery when he leaves. Speculate on what might have happened to him in the past and what the future may hold for him.

♣ Shane tells Bob that "a gun is just a tool." Debate this statement.

♣ Read Robert Frost's "The Road Not Taken." Discuss its relevance to Shane's decision to take the road leading to the Starrett farm, rather than the road to Fletcher's ranch.

♣ Using the reports from the activity below, discuss whether or not the gunfighters in novels and movies are accurately portrayed.

♣ After reading the novel, watch the movie version of *Shane.* Discuss the following questions:
- Are there any differences between the novel and the movie? What are they?
- Did you find the movie or the novel to be more realistic? Why?
- Did the actors give convincing portrayals of the characters?
- Was the movie set effective?
- Did you change your opinion of any of the characters after seeing them in the movie?

♣ Prepare a report comparing the cattle industry of today with cattle raising of a hundred years ago.

♣ Research an historical gunfighter and compare and contrast him with the character of Shane.

♣ Find out about the Homestead Act of 1862 and how it affected the development of the West. Discuss.

Date _____ Name _____

VOCABULARY

from the novel *Shane*

* *

Define the underlined word in each sentence.

1. Something <u>intangible</u> and cold and terrifying was there in the air between us.

_____

2. Father said it in a <u>musing</u> way.

_____

3. Shane turned to mother and his voice took on a <u>bantering</u> tone.

_____

4. We were, in some <u>subtle</u> way, Shane's folks.

_____

5. Father and Shane argued long and <u>amiably</u> about the cattle business.

_____

6. I wondered how all the slow-climbing tenseness in our valley could be so focused on one man and he seemed to be so <u>indifferent</u> to it.

_____

7. "You're a <u>discerning</u> woman, Marian. "

_____

8. "So-o-o-o," said Wilson, stretching out the word with <u>ominous</u> softness.

_____

9. Shane was tall and terrible there in the road, forging his lone way out of an unknown past in the utter loneliness of his own immovable and instinctive <u>defiance</u>.

_____

10. Wilson's voice, lazy and <u>insolent</u>, floated down the room.

_____

from the novel *Shane*

* *

Define the underlined word in each sentence.

11. Father and the stranger measured each other in an unspoken <u>fraternity</u> of adult knowledge beyond my reach.

_____

12. Father grunted in <u>exasperation</u>.

_____

13. Shane and my parents were enjoying themselves even though I could feel a bit of <u>constraint</u> behind the easy joshing.

_____

14. The <u>recurrent</u> trouble between Fletcher and us homesteaders seemed to have faded away.

_____

15. The other people of the valley still thought of us homesteaders as there by Fletcher's <u>sufferance</u>.

_____

16. Shane had lost the <u>serenity</u> that had seeped into him through the summer.

_____

17. The <u>lithe</u> power in Shane was singing in every fiber of him.

_____

18. Fletcher was smiling and <u>affable</u>.

_____

19. Shane's voice was even more gentle, but it had a quiet, <u>inflexible</u> quality that had never been there before.

_____

20. The folks in town and the kids at school liked to <u>speculate</u> about Shane.

_____

Date_____   Name_____

SHANE
CROSSWORD PUZZLE

Use what you have learned from the novel to complete the puzzle. Many of the words are taken from the vocabulary study.

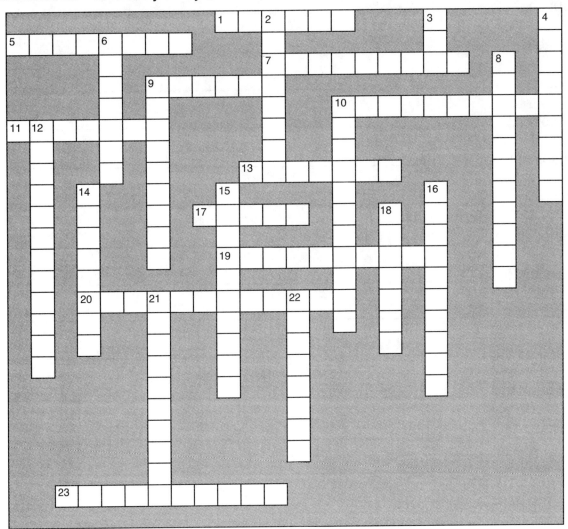

ACROSS

1. meditative
5. challenge
7. periodic
9. not immediately obvious
10. unable to be touched
11. friendly
13. state which is setting for novel
17. agile
19. embarrassment
20. annoyance
23. rigid

DOWN

2. peace
3. Shane doesn't carry one
4. teasing
6. in a friendly manner
8. he tells the story (two words)
9. ponder or reflect
10. disinterested
12. Joe warns Bob that Shane is this
14. insulting
15. perceptive
16. brotherhood
18. foreboding
21. consent
22. kind of stump that Joe and Shane wrestle with

15

Date_____   Name _____

PART I: VOCABULARY (20 points)
Write the definition of the word in the space next to it.

1. subtle _____

2. affable _____

3. exasperation _____

4. musing _____

5. insolent _____

6. amiably _____

7. serenity _____

8. speculate _____

9. indifferent _____

10. intangible _____

11. fraternity _____

12. lithe _____

13. inflexible _____

14. bantering _____

15. sufferance _____

16. discerning _____

17. recurrent _____

18. constraint _____

19. defiance _____

20. ominous _____

PART II: TRUE OR FALSE (10 points)

In the space provided, write *true* if the statement is completely true, or write *false* if any part of the statement is false.

_____ 1. Joe Starrett is friendly toward Shane when they first meet.

_____ 2. Bob is puzzled as to why Shane does not wear a gun.

_____ 3. Once Shane becomes comfortable with the Starretts, he tells them about his past.

_____ 4. Joe Starrett is regarded as a leader by the other homesteaders in the valley.

_____ 5. Both Shane and Joe Starrett never wear a gun.

_____ 6. Shane believes a gun is an evil thing.

_____ 7. Joe is convinced that Shane could take better care of his family than he can.

_____ 8. Joe tells Bob that he should learn to love Shane like a brother.

_____ 9. Shane is seriously wounded by Stark Wilson in the gunfight at Grafton's.

_____ 10. Marian Starrett is frightened by Shane; she believes him to be a threat to her family.

PART III: MULTIPLE CHOICE (30 points)

Decide which is the best response for each of the following sentences. Write the letter of your choice in the space provided.

_____ 1. Shane is friendly when he first meets the Starretts, but he is reluctant:
    (a) to stay for supper
    (b) to talk about raising cattle
    (c) to concern himself with the conflict between Fletcher and the homesteaders
    (d) to discuss his past

_____ 2. Joe Starrett believes that running cattle in big lots on open range is:
    (a) a profitable idea for big ranchers, but not for him
    (b) the best way to raise cattle, but not practical now that homesteaders are fencing the open range
    (c) doomed because it produces little profit and uses too much space
    (d) profitable, provided the railroad is close enough to use for shipping cattle to market

_____ 3. Joe might have used a team of horses to finish pulling out the ironwood stump, but he didn't because he and Shane wanted to:
(a) impress Marian
(b) prove that they were very strong
(c) prove that man can win a battle over a stubborn adversary
(d) establish their friendship and partnership

_____ 4. Joe advised Bob not to like Shane too much because Shane is:
(a) fiddle-footed
(b) dangerous
(c) a gunfighter
(d) lazy

_____ 5. Shane believes Chris:
(a) is stupid and foolish
(b) has the makings of a man
(c) is arrogant and a bully
(d) will probably become a gunfighter

_____ 6. Shane's final words of advice to Bob include all but one of the following:
(a) grow up strong and straight
(b) go home to his mother and father
(c) take care of his mother and father
(d) stay away from guns and killing

_____ 7. Shane leaves the valley because:
(a) he knows he is dying from his wounds
(b) there is no going back from killing
(c) the sheriff is going to arrest him for murder
(d) if he stays he will have to keep killing Fletcher's men

_____ 8. Shane finally decides to strap on his gun because:
(a) Wilson forced him to
(b) he wants to prove to Bob that he is courageous
(c) he is in love with Marian and wants to kill Joe
(d) he loves the Starretts like his own family and wants to protect them

_____ 9. The novel, *Shane*, is written from the point of view of:
(a) an adult remembering the past
(b) a young boy
(c) the author
(d) Shane

_____ 10. When Shane first rides into the valley, it is clear that he is:
(a) an escaped convict
(b) trying to escape his violent past
(c) hoping to get married and settle down
(d) looking for a steady job

_____ 11. Joe and Shane's struggle with the ironwood stump symbolizes:
   (a) their friendship
   (b) man's struggle to dominate nature
   (c) the conflict between the Starretts and Fletcher
   (d) Shane's love for his new family

_____ 12. Joe never asks Shane why he keeps a gun hidden in his saddle-roll because:
   (a) he's afraid Shane will kill him
   (b) he doesn't care
   (c) he respects Shane too much to ask
   (d) he doesn't want to worry Marian and Bob

_____ 13. Shane tells Bob that a gun is:
   (a) just a tool
   (b) an evil weapon
   (c) man's best friend
   (d) a symbol of a real man

_____ 14. Which of the following does Fletcher NOT offer Joe Starrett for his land?
   (a) twelve hundred dollars
   (b) the job of foreman on his ranch
   (c) the opportunity to continue working his own land
   (d) a partnership in his cattle business

_____ 15. After the gunfight with Wilson and Fletcher, Shane is convinced that he:
   (a) cannot escape his gunfighter past
   (b) was wrong to get involved
   (c) should have taken the road to the Fletcher ranch instead of the Starretts'
   (d) should leave the valley before more people get killed

PART IV: ESSAY (40 points)
Answer <u>two</u> of the following essay questions.

1. Trace the development of the relationship between the Starrett family and Shane.

2. What did Shane mean when he said, "A man is what he is, and there's no breaking the mold"?

3. What were Shane's internal and external conflicts, and how did he resolve each of them?

4. Joe said, "Shane won his fight before he ever came riding into this valley." Explain what he meant by that.

19

ANSWER KEY

Answers to Word Study (page 6)

1. range: land where cattle are raised
2. mythical: fictional
3. graze: nibble at grass in a pasture
4. homesteaders: families who accepted U.S. land grants and built homes on them
5. stereotyped: a standard conception about something
6. suspense: a state of uncertainly, excitement
7. challenge: an invitation to fight, or a dare
8. economic: financial
9. hothead: a quick-tempered person
10. confrontation: a defiant, face to face encounter

Answers to Anticipation Guide (page 7)

1. Bob Starrett
2. slender, graceful but with a deadly look about him, good with fists and gun, decent and honorable, larger than life character, well-groomed
3. Fletcher's men roughed him up and scared him off
4. He wants more land on which to run his cattle
5. He takes Joe Starrett and the homesteaders' side

Answers to Word Search (page 8)

1. BOB
2. CONFRONTATION
3. GUNFIGHTER
4. JACK SCHAEFER
5. STARK WILSON
6. WEST
7. CATTLEMEN
8. ECONOMIC
9. HOMESTEADERS
10. MYTHICAL
11. STEREOTYPED
12. CHALLENGE
13. GRAZE
14. HOTHEAD
15. RANGE
16. SUSPENSE

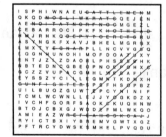

Answers to Questions for Study and Discussion

Literal Level (page 9)

1. Starrett farm or at Grafton's place, Wyoming; summer of 1889.
2. He was run off by Fletcher.
3. An ivory-handled Colt revolver
4. Stark Wilson

5. He is goaded into a gunfight by Stark Wilson, who kills him.
6. He knocks Joe unconscious.
7. Stark Wilson and Fletcher
8. He rides out of the valley forever.

Interpretive Level (page 10)

1. Fletcher believed that cattle should be run in large lots on the open range. Joe Starrett felt this was wasteful and an inefficient use of the land. He said "Put in enough crops to carry you and make your money play with a small herd, not all horns and bone, but bred for meat and fenced in and fed right." In fact, by 1889 ranchers were abandoning the open range method for the very reasons that Joe gave.

2. The stump is the one thing on the Starrett farm that Joe has been unable to conquer. His struggle to remove it may symbolize man's attempts to dominate nature. Shane attacks the stump with an ax, acknowledging Joe's confidence in his integrity. Together, the men struggle with the stump, creating a bond of respect and affection which foreshadows their developing close friendship.

3. Early in the novel he demonstrates great skill in handling a gun.

4. Because he has too much respect for Shane.

5. Because he thinks of Chris as a courageous young man who was only doing what he had been told.

Critical Level (page 11)

1. Shane's internal battle probably involves his decision to no longer wear a gun.

2. Bob and Joe are common names, representing the strengths and virtues of common men who live by the land. Shane is an exotic name, representing the mysterious nature of the character. "Stark" is defined as barren, cold, desolate.

3. Their reasons for fighting are never clearly defined, but it may be assumed that their fight was for more than just the land; it included maintaining their pride, protecting their home, establishing rights for common people.

ANSWER KEY

Answers to Crossword Puzzle (page 15)

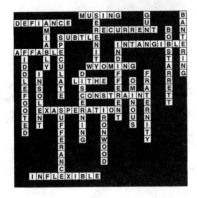

Answers to Test

PART I: VOCABULARY (page 16)

1. subtle
    (not immediately obvious)
2. affable
    (friendly)
3. exasperation
    (annoyance)
4. musing
    (meditative)
5. insolent
    (insulting)
6. amiably
    (in a friendly manner)
7. serenity
    (peace)
8. speculate
    (ponder or reflect)
9. indifferent
    (disinterested)
10. intangible
    (unable to be touched)
11. fraternity
    (brotherhood)
12. lithe
    (agile)
13. inflexible
    (rigid)
14. bantering
    (teasing)
15. sufferance
    (consent)
16. discerning
    (perceptive)

17. recurrent
    (periodic)
18. constraint
    (embarrassment)
19. defiance
    (challenge)
20. ominous
    (foreboding)

PART II: TRUE OR FALSE (page 17)

1. true
2. true
3. false
4. true
5. false
6. false
7. true
8. false
9. true
10. false

PART III: MULTIPLE CHOICE (page 17-19)

1. D
2. C
3. C
4. A
5. B
6. D
7. B
8. D
9. A
10. B
11. B
12. C
13. A
14. D
15. A

PART IV: ESSAY (page 19)
Answers will vary.

SOUNDER

by William H. Armstrong

SYNOPSIS

It is colder and windier than usual this winter. The road past the sharecropper's cabin is hard and frozen, and bare branches of trees click against each other in the wind. Hunting is poor. Each night the boy sees his father and the great 'coon dog, Sounder, return with an empty bag. Maybe the raccoons and 'possums have all gone farther south.

Then one morning the boy wakes up to the smell of pork sausages and ham bone. That's better than stew 'possum anytime, and a whole lot better than the little bit of corn mush they've had to get by on everyday. But the good feeling doesn't last long.

Three days later, the men come—the sheriff and his deputies—to take the boy's father away because he stole the ham and sausage from the landowner's smokehouse. Not even Sounder can stop them, but he tries.

First his father taken away, then Sounder shot. No, the good feeling didn't last long.

He was an old, grey-haired black man–the man who told William Armstrong the story of Sounder, back when Armstrong was a small boy. It was from this old man that Armstrong learned to read, as he informs us in an author's note. And also from this old man, the little boy heard stories—stories out of the Bible, out of ancient Greek classics, history, and one story out of the old man's own life, when he was a boy. That story is *Sounder.*

As Armstrong, fifty years later, retells the story in novel form, it has a poetic quality, though written in simple prose. Short for a novel, it can be read quickly, but it is full of symbols, and many persons will be moved to read it a second time. It is essentially the story of human beings under oppression, yet not only keeping the best of their human qualities whole, but enlarging and building upon them.

The setting is the nineteenth century South, after the Civil War and Reconstruction period. Times were hard in most parts of the region—hardest for blacks and poor whites. The South was an agricultural region before the Civil War—a devastating war fought mostly on southern land—and most Southerners went back to agriculture after the war. Not only was there physical devastation, but there was little cash available, even to large landowners. For blacks, newly-freed from slavery, and poor whites, there was no access to credit, either. So a system of tenant farming by sharecropping was created. Landowners liked it because they didn't have to pay out much cash to farm labor. People who had nothing to sell but their labor liked the system, too, at first. Sharecroppers got a share of the harvest, usually a fourth, with three-fourths going to the landowner. Plus, sharecroppers got cabins in which to live, tools, seed, and often food. The problem was that as this system developed, the sharecropper's one-fourth share was seldom enough to do more than cover debts at the local store, if that. In addition, the crop might be bad. There was a series of bad crops right after the war and a widespread farm depression in the 1870's. In the 1890's, southern farmers were hit especially hard by the drastic fall of crop prices. Too often when the crop was in, a sharecropper's family, like the family in *Sounder,* was left with nothing to get them through the winter, unless the hunting was good.

White officials in *Sounder* —like the sheriff, his deputies, and the jailer—are characterized as brutal men. Not all such officials were brutal, of course, but many were, where blacks were concerned. Put the black man in his place and keep him there, by whatever methods necessary—that seemed to be the goal of southern white society, beginning in the Reconstruction period. To accomplish that end, white terrorist groups, which in some places included local sheriffs, mounted a wave of violence in the late 1860's and into the 1870's. Known collectively as the Ku Klux Klan, the terrorists whipped, maimed, and murdered both blacks and whites who protected them, in addition to burning black churches and newly-created black schools. Finally, a reluctant federal government was forced to take a hand, and eventually large-scale violence subsided, but not before the Klan accomplished its purpose of intimidating southern blacks.

Individual cases of lynchings and beatings of blacks continued right on up into the twentieth century, while blacks were systematically deprived of their right to vote and subjected to Jim Crow laws. Not until the Civil Rights movement of the 1960's did the situation change in the South. But it did change, to the point where a number of southern communities now have black mayors. Also, as southern agriculture has become more and more mechanized, sharecropping and the tenant farm system have been disappearing. Yet, even now there are places where the nineteenth century world of *Sounder* is still the twentieth century reality. Places where women like the mother in *Sounder* are only too glad to get what money they can from doing laundry for the people who live in the big houses in town. She will have to take in more laundry and gather even more walnuts to sell at the store, now that there is no man in the house to go hunting and no coon hound to hunt with.

Sounder limped off in the road where he had been shot. He wasn't killed, after all, but he was badly wounded. Maybe he has gone off into the woods to heal himself—or to die. Once the boy goes into the woods to look for Sounder, but he doesn't find the dog, and when he comes home he is so chilled his mother tells him not to go out again. He has got to learn to lose, she tells him. But he is not the type to be a loser. What he really wants to learn is how to read. And he wants to know what has happened to his father.

One day Sounder comes home. He's terribly crippled and almost starving, and he will never hunt again. But he is alive, and he is home.

One day, too, the boy's mother brings back word of his father. The judge has sentenced him to hard labor. He will be on a chain gang, moving from place to place around the state.

As time passes, the boy feels a great need to go in search of his father, and he sets out on the first of many journeys to road camps and prison farms and quarries around the state.

The boy does not find his father, but he learns. He learns about people and places, and he learns how to read from old newspapers and magazines. Once he finds a large book

23

with part of its cover missing. In it are words and ideas that the boy doesn't yet understand, but which in time he will. These words and ideas—and more.

After being gone most of each winter, the boy returns home before planting time to work in the field so his mother and brother and sisters can continue to live in the cabin. Each time the boy returns, he can see from far off the dog, Sounder, hobbling down the road to meet him. And always there is the hope that one day, along this same road, the boy's father, too, will return.

Do you think the father will ever return? Read the rest of the novel to find out!

BIBLIOGRAPHY

Ethridge, James and Barbara Kopala (ed.), *Comtemporary Authors*, Vols. 19-20. Detroit: Gale Research, 1965.

Reviews:
Best Sellers, November 1, 1969, p. 305.
Christian Science Monitor, November 6, 1969, p. B9.
Commonweal, November 21, 1969, p. 257.
Horn Book, December, 1969, p. 673.
Library Journal, December 15, 1969, p. 4610.
New York Times Book Review, October 16, 1969, p. 42.
Saturday Review, December 20, 1969, p. 30.

WILLIAM H. ARMSTRONG

Born in Lexington, Virginia, in 1914, William H. Armstrong attended Augusta Military Academy from 1928 to 1932, and he graduated cum laude from Hampden-Sydney College in 1936. He began a long career as history master at Kent School, Kent, Connecticut, in 1945. In 1963 he was awarded the National School Bell Award of the National Association of School Administrators for distinguished service in the interpretation of education.

Armstrong was a skillful writer at an early age, although he had difficulty in convincing some of his school teachers of that. As a student at Augusta Military Academy, he was given an assignment to write an original story for his English composition class. He wrote an intriguing story about a crippled boy who gazed out of a window at the apple orchard where he could never run and play. After the class ended, the instructor asked young Armstrong to stay behind, and then demanded to know from where he had copied his story. Neither the instructor, the head of the English department, nor the headmaster of the school could be convinced that it was an original story. Armstrong made the decision that from that day on he would only write conventional stories, like the other students'. But once he entered college, he submitted the story of the crippled boy to the school's literary magazine, and it was published.

He won the John Newbery Medal for *Sounder,* which was published in 1969 and later made into a successful motion picture. In addition to *Sounder,* Armstrong has written several books concerning study skills. Among them are *Study is Hard Work* (1956; 2nd edition 1967), *87 Ways to Help Your Child in School* (1961), and *Tools of Thinking* (1968). He has also written several history books, including *The Peoples of the Ancient World* (1959), and *Hadassah: Esther, the Orphan Queen* (1972).

William H. Armstrong lives in Connecticut in a house he built himself. He raises Corriedale sheep and claims to prefer stone masonry and carpentry to writing.

Bibliography
Something About the Author, Vol. 4. New York: Gale Research Co., 1973.

Date _____ Name _____

AUTHOR PROFILE

Some of the answers to the following questions may be found in the biography on the preceding page. For other information, check your library.

AUTHOR'S NAME :   *William H. Armstrong*

1. What has this author written?_____

_____

2. Date of birth _____ Date of death _____

3. What does/did this author look like? _____

_____

_____

4. Where did this author grow up? _____

5. Did this author have any particular difficulties in his life? What were they?

_____

_____

6. What kinds of things does/did this author like to write about most? _____

_____

7. What kind of education does/did this author have? _____

8. What kinds of jobs did this author hold?_____

9. What did you find to be particularly interesting when reading about this author's life?

_____

_____

10. If you could talk to this author in person, what would you like to ask him?

_____

Date _____ Name _____

WORD STUDY

Define the underlined words:

1. The road past the <u>sharecropper</u>'s cabin is hard and frozen . . .

_____

2. It is essentially the story of human beings under <u>oppression</u> . . .

_____

3. Not only was there physical <u>devastation</u>, but there was little cash available, even to large landowners.

_____

4. For blacks, newly-freed from slavery, and poor whites, there was no <u>access</u> to credit, either.

_____

5. So a system of <u>tenant</u> farming by sharecropping was created.

_____

6. . . . . . the sharecropper's one-fourth share was seldom enough to do more than cover <u>debts</u> at the local store, if that.

_____

7. There was a series of bad crops right after the war and a widespread farm <u>depression</u> in the 1870's.

_____

8. White officials in *Sounder*—like the sheriff, his deputies, and the jailer—are characterized as <u>brutal</u> men.

_____

9. To accomplish that end, white <u>terrorist</u> groups, which in some places included local sheriffs, mounted a wave of violence in the late 1860's and into the 1870's.

_____

10. . . . .eventually large-scale violence subsided, but not before the Klan accomplished its purpose of <u>intimidating</u> southern blacks.

_____

27

Date _____ Name _____

(ANTICIPATION GUIDE)

for the novel *Sounder*

The numbered questions can be answered from reading the synopsis for the novel. Express your own thoughts when answering the questions that are marked with a ⟹.

1. Why is the father taken to jail? _____

_____

⟹Considering his crime, do you think the father's punishment was too easy or too severe? Why?

_____

_____

2. What happens to Sounder when the father is taken away? _____

_____

_____

⟹Why do you suppose the author chose to name the book after the dog?

_____

_____

3. In what places does the boy go in search of his father? _____

_____

⟹Do you think it is wise or foolish for a young boy to go to these places? Why?

_____

_____

4. What does the boy learn as he travels in search of his father? _____

_____

⟹Why do you think it is so important to him to learn these things? _____

_____

5. Who comes to meet the boy each time he returns home? _____

⟹Do you think the boy's father will ever return? _____

Date _____ Name _____

SOUNDER
Word Search

Using the clues below, find the answers hidden in the puzzle and circle them. They may be printed horizontally, vertically, diagonally, or backward. All of the words are associated with the novel in some way.

```
I  H  U  M  A  X  Z  B  N  T  L  A  U  N  D  R  Y  R  C  X
H  P  X  P  S  O  U  T  H  K  E  Z  S  D  G  X  L  Z  X  U
X  W  B  S  Q  D  L  I  W  K  L  R  A  T  K  I  J  W  P  O
D  W  I  I  H  U  V  V  C  L  X  A  R  U  D  F  J  D  M  W
I  B  G  N  U  A  O  X  Z  Y  O  K  T  O  F  S  I  E  C  E
I  R  B  T  T  W  R  G  A  Y  J  O  Y  U  R  F  B  V  X  Z
Q  C  E  P  S  I  T  E  N  A  N  T  D  F  R  I  K  A  E  X
J  B  I  A  I  D  M  Z  C  B  D  J  L  J  T  B  S  S  T  Z
J  S  V  F  D  C  O  I  W  R  Q  V  I  I  L  P  V  T  N  D
J  P  C  Z  C  P  P  C  D  P  O  Z  U  R  Y  L  X  A  B  F
G  U  I  Z  L  D  P  R  W  A  P  P  Z  E  Z  S  H  T  C  R
J  I  U  Z  F  C  R  J  G  D  T  I  P  Y  P  D  W  I  A  G
S  S  E  C  C  A  E  L  L  L  L  I  W  E  Q  I  V  O  K  K
H  A  M  W  K  B  S  I  Y  N  V  W  N  W  R  D  Q  N  T  A
D  H  X  N  V  Z  S  P  R  S  J  B  N  G  N  R  H  W  V  H
I  B  W  I  L  L  I  A  M  H  A  R  M  S  T  R  O  N  G  I
D  I  E  B  G  C  O  U  X  I  T  E  O  Y  T  P  E  F  H  I
A  Z  G  A  R  R  N  Z  N  Z  I  Z  V  A  D  F  S  E  Z  C
D  X  R  C  H  E  G  Z  S  T  B  E  D  P  U  J  E  A  R  J
C  G  F  A  D  E  P  R  E  S  S  I  O  N  R  I  O  D  D  D
```

1. to get
2. things that are owed to someone
3. something the father stole
4. cruel or unjust restrictions imposed by authority figures
5. geographical setting of *Sounder*
6. author of *Sounder*
7. very cruel
8. a period of slow business and unemployment

9. causing fear
10. what the boy learned to do on his journeys
11. a renter
12. kind of home the family lived in
13. overwhelming destruction
14. kind of work the mother did
15. a farmer who pays a share of his crop as rent
16. someone who uses force or cruelty to intimidate

29

Date _____ Name _____

QUESTIONS FOR STUDY AND DISCUSSION

for the novel *Sounder*

Literal Level

1. Sounder is the only character in the book who is named. Why is he named "Sounder"?

_____

_____

_____

2. Why is the father arrested? How does the sheriff find him, and what is his punishment?

_____

_____

_____

3. Who shoots Sounder? Why? How badly is Sounder injured?

_____

_____

_____

4. What is it that the boy wishes the people his mother works for would give her? Why is it so important to him?

_____

_____

_____

5. What happens to Sounder's voice?

_____

_____

_____

Date _____ Name _____

QUESTIONS FOR STUDY AND DISCUSSION

for the novel *Sounder*

Interpretive Level

1. How is the boy treated by white people? What is his reaction to this treatment?

_____

_____

_____

_____

_____

2. Is the boy's search for his father a success or a failure? Explain.

_____

_____

_____

_____

3. How long is it before the father returns? Has he changed at all during the time he has been on the chain gang? Explain.

_____

_____

_____

_____

Date _____ Name _____

QUESTIONS FOR STUDY AND DISCUSSION

for the novel *Sounder*

Critical Level

1. In a note preceding the novel, the author compares Sounder with the dog Argus from *The Odyssey.* In your opinion, is this a valid comparison? Explain.

_____

_____

_____

_____

_____

2. It is unusual for the characters in a book to remain unnamed. Why do you think the author has chosen to do this in *Sounder*?

_____

_____

_____

_____

_____

3. The boy finds a book of essays by Montaigne which greatly influence his life. Is there a book which you have read that has had a similar influence on your life? Explain.

_____

_____

_____

_____

_____

ACTIVITIES

for the novel *Sounder*

♣ Using pictures and drawings, design a bulletin board display depicting the changing status of black Americans from slavery to modern times, particularly in the South.

♣ Report on how a particular book has influenced your life.

♣ The setting for the novel, *Sounder*, is approximately one hundred years ago. Do you think a story like this could be set in America today? Write an essay defending your position.

♣ Debate this question: Who suffers the greatest harm from racial discrimination—the persecuted, the persecutors, or the innocent bystanders?

♣ Imagine that you are the boy in the novel. Write a letter to the black teacher who has befriended you, telling him about the death of your father and your dog.

♣ Read other books about the black experience in the South, such as Richard Wright's *Black Boy*. Write a paper comparing and contrasting this book with *Sounder*.

Date _____ Name _____

(VOCABULARY)

from the novel *Sounder*
* *

Define the underlined word in each sentence.

1. It <u>mellowed</u> into half-echo before it touched the air.

_____

2. ". . . you'll make the creatures <u>skittish</u>."

_____

3. Under the cabin it smelled stale and dead, like old <u>carcasses</u> and snakes.

_____

4. ". . . he might be <u>addled</u> crazy and not know where he wandered off to die."

_____

5. ". . . act <u>perkish</u> and don't grieve your father."

_____

6. . . . the crippled coon dog would <u>hobble</u> far down the road to meet him . . .

_____

7. His arm swung in apelike <u>gyrations</u> of glee . . .

_____

8. "I have found by experience that <u>malicious</u> and inhuman . . ."

_____

9. ". . . <u>animosity</u> and fierceness are usually accomplished by weakness."

_____

10. "He's <u>conjured</u>," the boy whispered to himself.

_____

VOCABULARY

from the novel *Sounder*
* *

Define the underlined word in each sentence.

11. There was another yelp, this one <u>constrained</u> and

_____

12. <u>plaintive</u>.

_____

13. The tears ran down through the cobwebs and dust that covered his face, making little <u>rivulets</u>.

_____

14. In the matted Scotch-broom tangle he <u>visualized</u> the great tan body . . .

_____

15. The town and the jail seemed to become more <u>remote</u>.

_____

16. She seemed to understand the <u>compulsion</u> that started him on each long, fruitless journey with new hope.

_____

17. . . . the boy had not run but had stood still and <u>defiant</u>.

_____

18. . . . the boy had learned to sniff out danger and spot <u>orneriness</u> quickly.

_____

19. Just when the <u>commotion</u> was quieting down, a man appeared at the schoolhouse door.

_____

20. "Read somethin' from the <u>Scriptures</u>."

_____

Date _____ Name _____

SOUNDER
CROSSWORD PUZZLE

Use what you have learned from the novel to complete the puzzle. Many of the words are taken from the vocabulary study.

ACROSS

1. bearing ill will
6. author of essays found by the boy
7. unnatural
11. circulations
14. Sounder's distinctive characteristic
16. bewitched
19. mournful
21. nastiness
22. nervous
23. the father's punishment was to work on one (two words)
24. rebellious

DOWN

1. softened
2. uproar
3. it blew up and injured the father
4. occupation of man who befriends the boy
5. limp
8. hatred
9. bodies
10. emotional pressure
12. distant
13. confused
15. Bible
17. streams
18. imagined
20. jaunty

Sounder- Test

Date _____ Name _____

PART I: VOCABULARY (20 points)
Write the definition of the word in the space next to it.

1. orneriness _____

2. conjured _____

3. carcasses _____

4. visualized _____

5. Scriptures _____

6. gyrations _____

7. perkish _____

8. mellowed _____

9. constrained _____

10. remote _____

11. hobble _____

12. skittish _____

13. rivulets _____

14. commotion _____

15. plaintive _____

16. addled _____

17. malicious _____

18. animosity _____

19. compulsion _____

20. defiant _____

PART II: TRUE OR FALSE (10 points)

In the space provided, write *true* if the statement is completely true, or write *false* if any part of the statement is false.

_____ 1. The boy is the youngest member of his family.

_____ 2. The father plans to sell the food he steals.

_____ 3. The boy doesn't go to school because the school is too far away.

_____ 4. The boy doesn't like the endings of most Bible stories.

_____ 5. The boy finally finds his father working in a prison quarry.

_____ 6. The sheriff arrests the boy's father, even though he has no evidence against him.

_____ 7. The boy finds a part of Sounder's ear in the road.

_____ 8. The white-haired black man tells the boy that since Montaigne lived in the 1500's, his essays have little relevance to the boy's life.

_____ 9. The boy's mother reads Bible stories to him.

_____ 10. When the father returns home from prison, Sounder acts like a young dog again.

PART III: MULTIPLE CHOICE (30 points)

Decide which is the best response for each of the following sentences. Write the letter of your choice in the space provided.

_____ 1. The most extraordinary characteristic about Sounder is:
(a) his size
(b) his bad temper
(c) his voice
(d) his intelligence

_____ 2. The boy's mother only hums when she is:
(a) happy
(b) worried
(c) sad
(d) washing dishes

_____ 3. The boy's mother tells him that the wounded Sounder has probably:
(a) gone off to die
(b) gone off to heal himself
(c) gone to search for the father
(d) gone to find someone who will take better care of him

_____ 4. The father tells his son:
       (a) to never visit him in jail again
       (b) to hide a hacksaw blade in a cake
       (c) to find Sounder
       (d) to go to school

_____ 5. Not hearing from his father, the boy decides to:
       (a) go search for him
       (b) take care of his mother
       (c) go to school
       (d) leave home forever

_____ 6. When he was in a strange town, what did the boy find in a trash barrel?
       (a) food
       (b) clothing
       (c) a newspaper containing a story about his father
       (d) a book of essays

_____ 7. The father became crippled because:
       (a) he was beaten by a prison guard
       (b) he was shot trying to escape
       (c) he was wounded in a knife fight with another prisoner
       (d) he was injured in a dynamite blast

_____ 8. Sounder:
       (a) dies the same day his master dies
       (b) dies shortly after his master's funeral
       (c) lives for several years after his master dies
       (d) does not die in the story

_____ 9. The black family in the novel reacts to oppression by:
       (a) seeking revenge
       (b) enduring with simple dignity
       (c) refusing to work
       (d) living in fear

_____ 10. The literary style of *Sounder* can best be described as:
       (a) complex and difficult
       (b) wordy and flowery
       (c) vulgar and common
       (d) stark and simple

_____ 11. At the jail, the red-faced man:
       (a) tells the boy to go away
       (b) calls the boy a sissy
       (c) hits the boy
       (d) crumbles the cake that the boy has brought for his father

_____ 12. A prison guard:
       (a) throws the boy across the room
       (b) invites the boy to share his lunch
       (c) smashes the boy's fingers with a piece of iron
       (d) teaches the boy how to read

_____ 13. The father dies:
        (a) in a dynamite explosion
        (b) in the deep pine woods
        (c) in jail
        (d) while plowing in the field

_____ 14. The boy wants to learn to read because:
        (a) books can open up a new world of experience for him
        (b) his parents want him to read to them
        (c) he wants to be a teacher
        (d) he can't get a job unless he can read

_____ 15. The main theme of *Sounder* is:
        (a) a poor family can never hope to get ahead
        (b) black people will always be oppressed
        (c) although life may be grim and tragic, one may still grow and find
            fulfillment
        (d) hard work always pays off

PART IV: ESSAY (40 points)

Answer <u>two</u> of the following essay questions.

1. Describe the ways that the black family responds to persecution and tragedy.

2. Explain why it is so important to the boy to read and learn. Do you think his obsession is believable? Why or why not?

3. Describe how the boy changes as a result of his experiences.

4. Do you think *Sounder* has a happy or tragic ending? Defend your position.

ANSWER KEY

Answers to Word Study (page 27)

1. sharecropper: a farmer who pays a share of his crop as rent
2. oppression: cruel or unjust restrictions imposed by authority figures
3. devastation: overwhelming destruction
4. access: to get
5. tenant: a renter
6. debts: things that are owed to someone
7. depression: a period of slow business and unemployment
8. brutal: very cruel
9. terrorist: someone who uses force or cruelty to intimidate
10. intimidating: causing fear

Answers to Anticipation Guide (page 28)

1. He stole ham and sausages from the landowner
2. He is shot, but not killed; he goes into the woods to heal himself and later returns
3. road camps, prison farms, quarries
4. He learns about people and places, and how to read
5. Sounder

Answers to Word Search (page 29)

1. ACCESS
2. DEBTS
3. HAM
4. OPPRESSION
5. SOUTH
6. WILLIAM H. ARMSTRONG
7. BRUTAL
8. DEPRESSION
9. INTIMIDATING
10. READ
11. TENANT
12. CABIN
13. DEVASTATION
14. LAUNDRY
15. SHARECROPPER
16. TERRORIST

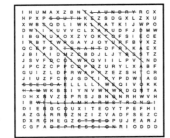

Answers to Questions for Study and Discussion
Literal Level (page 30)

1. Sounder is named for his bark, which "came out of the great chest cavity and broad jaws as though it had bounced off the walls of a cave," and "mellowed into half-echo before it touched the air." The passage from which this quote is taken should be particularly noted for its rich imagery.

2. The father is arrested for stealing a ham from a white man's smokehouse in order to feed his hungry family. The sheriff is able to track him because of a piece of the father's overalls which had torn from his clothes and was found on the smokehouse door hook. He is sentenced to hard labor on the chain gang–a severe punishment in light of the nature of the crime, but not uncommon in the American South of the nineteenth century.

3. When the sheriff is ready to drive away with the boy's father in chains in his wagon, he warns the boy to hold Sounder if he doesn't want him dead. Sounder is shot after he breaks away from the boy's grasp and lunges at the wagon carrying the boy's father. The boy believes the dog to be dead, but later finds his body missing from the place in the road where he fell. His wounds are severe enough, however, that the boy's mother tells him that Sounder has probably crawled away to find a place to die.

4. The boy wishes his mother's employers would give her an old book. He is aware that his illiteracy will be a barrier to finding success and fulfillment in his life, and that education is the key to getting ahead.

5. After being injured by the shotgun blast, Sounder's magnificent bark is stilled. There is no physical reason for this silence, and when the father returns home Sounder's joy restores his great voice.

Interpretive Level (page 31)

1. The boy is physically and emotionally abused every time he encounters white people. The boy feels helpless and is enraged, and he fantasizes about revenge.

2. The search for his father is a failure, since the boy is never able to find him. However, in the course of his journeys he learns to read and meets the black teacher whose encouragement bolsters the boy's determination to gain knowledge and wisdom.

3. It is six years before the father returns home. He has suffered crippling injuries in a dynamite blast. But he has maintained his resolution to stay alive long enough to return home to see his family one last time.

ANSWER KEY

<u>Critical Level</u> (page 32)

1. In *The Odyssey*, Argus is Odysseus' dog, and the only one to recognize him when, disguised as a beggar, he returns home following an absence of twenty years. The two dogs may be seen as representative of several parallels between the two stories: the father's long absence; the boy's search for him; the wife's faithfulness; the dog's patient loyalty. Also, the main characters in both stories are heroes; but where Odysseus performed heroic deeds of monumental proportions, the black family in *Sounder* is heroic in their spiritual goodness and unshaken dignity.

2. Students' opinions may vary. Accept any reasonable answer.

3. Answers will vary.

Answers to Crossword Puzzle (page 36)

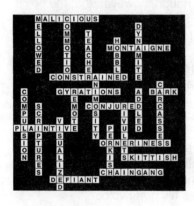

Answers to Test
PART I: VOCABULARY (page 37)

1. orneriness
   (nastiness)
2. conjured
   (bewitched)
3. carcasses
   (bodies)
4. visualized
   (imagined)
5. Scriptures
   (Bible)
6. gyrations
   (circulations)
7. perkish
   (jaunty)
8. mellowed
   (softened)
9. constrained
   (unnatural)
10. remote
    (distant)
11. hobble
    (limp)
12. skittish
    (nervous)
13. rivulets
    (streams)
14. commotion
    (uproar)
15. plaintive
    (mournful)
16. addled
    (confused)
17. malicious
    (bearing ill will)
18. animosity
    (hatred)
19. compulsion
    (emotional pressure)
20. defiant
    (rebellious)

PART II: TRUE OR FALSE (page 38)

1. false
2. false
3. true
4. false
5. false
6. false
7. true
8. false
9. false
10. true

PART III: MULTIPLE CHOICE (pages 38-40)

1. C	9. B
2. B	10. D
3. A	11. D
4. A	12. C
5. A	13. B
6. D	14. A
7. D	15. C
8. B	

PART IV: ESSAY (page 40)
Answers will vary.

THE OLD MAN AND THE SEA

by Ernest Hemingway

SYNOPSIS

On one level, it is a simple story—an old fisherman rows out to sea alone in an open boat. Far out. There he hooks a giant marlin which he struggles heroically to bring in to shore against tremendous odds. A simple story, dramatic and suspenseful. Yet, as crafted by Ernest Hemingway, it is rich with different levels of meaning. And it is a story in which we can see ourselves. For this is not only one old man testing himself beyond his limits. It is everyone—everyone who has dared a great thing.

The month is September, when the mighty ocean current called the Gulf Stream runs strong, rushing northeastward between Florida and Cuba. It is the time for big fish, the time for men of the fishing villages along the Cuban coast to make the most of each day. This is the setting for *The Old Man and the Sea* —a setting that Ernest Hemingway knew well. As a deep-sea fisherman himself, and having lived in Cuba for many years, he wrote from experience. Capturing for the reader the true quality of an experience and its physical setting was important to Hemingway in creating his fiction. "All good books are alike," he once said, "in that they are truer than if they had really happened. And after you are finished reading one, you will feel that all that happened to you. And afterwards it all belongs to you, the good and the bad, the ecstasy, the remorse and sorrow, the people and the places, and how the weather was."

The main characters in Hemingway's true but fictional world are individualists. They live by their own code, supported by their own strength of will. They are often called upon by their code to show courage and endurance, alone against a reality designed to defeat them. Such a person is Santiago, the main character in *The Old Man and the Sea.* He is, first of all, an old man, his skin weathered, his frame gaunt. He is still strong, but not what he had once been—perhaps as Hemingway saw himself becoming at the time he wrote the book. Only Santiago's eyes look young, clear, and bright, and undefeated, even though it had been a luckless summer for him—84 days without a fish. He lives alone in a small shack, his wife long since dead. A boy from the village helps him. Santiago had taught the boy to fish, but now the boy goes out with other fishermen. He has been forbidden by his father to go with Santiago because the old man's luck is bad. Yet the boy loves the old man and helps him.

Before dawn on the morning of the 85th day, Santiago sets forth again. This time he goes beyond where most of the village fishermen dare to go in their small skiffs. For although he may no longer have the strength of youth, yet, as he told the boy, he still has a confident spirit, together with experience and skill. Nevertheless, he is only one man, alone. A courageous man, but in Hemingway's fiction, such men often get broken by the powers that they challenge. Will that happen to Santiago?

In any case, by the time the sun rises he has his baits in the water, far out in the Gulf Stream, each bait at a different depth, hanging straight down from the green sticks used as bobbers. In the boat are reserve coils of line—enough to give a big fish more than 1800 feet, if necessary.

For hours the old man rows slowly with the current, watching the birds, which tell him where the fish are, and watching the clouds, which tell him what the weather will be. Suddenly, one of the bobber sticks goes under, and the old man takes the line lightly in his hand. He knows by the gentle pull what is happening—a marlin is nibbling at the bait. The old man lets him nibble; the fish stops, makes a turn, and begins to nibble again.

The line zips out. The fish has taken the bait whole with the hook inside. But it is still not the moment to set the hook. First, the fish must have time to eat the bait. Then the old man strikes. He strikes hard, with every bit of his strength, to set the hook well and solid. But the fish doesn't rise. The old man has to brace himself with the line against his back, as what he knows to be a huge fish tows the boat farther and farther out to sea. If he ties the line to the boat, the fish could break it. The old man must use his body to hold the line so he can give the fish more, but only when necessary. The long ordeal has begun.

Courage and endurance amid constant pain, past the point when the body seemingly has no strength left but the strength of the spirit inside—that is part of the Hemingway Code. The old man's struggle is not just with the great fish, but with himself. He forces his body to endure, and as always in the best of Hemingway's fiction, the details are realistic and exact. At times the old man must borrow memories from the past to help him in his struggle—memories of a day when he was not an old man and had the strength to spare. At least now he has the weather with him. September is a hurricane month, but the sky tells him there will be no hurricane.

Then, all at once he feels the fish coming up, rising out of the water as if to show the old man just how great a fish he is. And he *is* great—the largest marlin the old man has ever seen. He hopes the fish will jump again to take in air and thus be unable to go very deep. But there are no more jumps that day.

Another night, and the old man manages to sleep, despite the pressure of the line. As he sleeps he dreams of lions playing on the African beaches he saw as a young sailor.

Suddenly he is jerked awake, the line cutting his hand in back. The fish is making a rush. Then the marlin jumps again—and again, and again. The old man cannot see the jumps, but he can feel them, and he can feel the line cutting his hand.

By the next morning, the tired fish is beginning to circle the boat. Each circle allows the old man to haul in more line and bring the marlin closer. But Santiago is tired, too—so tired he feels faint. Will he kill the fish, or will the fish kill him? He is not sure he cares anymore. He has come to regard the fish as a brother, the two of them linked together in a necessary ritual of death. The fish is the nobler of the two, he admits. The old man is superior only because of tricks and intelligence. But finally the marlin is alongside. Then, with one last reserve of strength, willed up from somewhere, Santiago finds enough strength to drive in the harpoon. At last the fight is over. Now to lash the marlin to the boat, raise the sail, and catch the afternoon wind for land.

But now he must pay the price—the price for having gone too far out. It comes an hour after the fish has been secured to the boat. And the rest is tragedy.

Was it a sin to have killed the fish, his brother, so far out? Out where he could not reach land before the sharks came? He had done it for the money the fish would bring him, and he needed the money. But he had also done it for pride. He was, after all, a fisherman. Yes, he had pride, and he could still fight the sharks, and he *would* fight them. He would go on fighting them for as long as he had to.

Now, to find out what happens to Santiago, read the rest of the novel!

BIBLIOGRAPHY

Aldridge, John W., *Time to Murder and Create: The Contemporary Novel in Crisis.* New York: David McKay Co., Inc., 1966.

Beach, Joseph Warren, *American Fiction, 1920-1940.* New York: Russell & Russell, 1960.

Duffey, Bernard, J. *Modern American Literature.* New York: Holt, Reinhart and Winston, 1964.

Geismar, Maxwell, *American Moderns, From Rebellion to Conformity.* New York: Hill & Wang, 1958.

Heiney, Donald, *Barron's Simplified Approach to Ernest Hemingway.* Woodbury, New York: Barron's Educational Series, Inc., 1967.

Heiney, Donald, *Recent American Literature.* Woodbury, New York: Barron's Educational Series, Inc., 1958.

Fiedelson, Charles Jr. and Paul Brodtkorb, Jr., *Interpretations of American Literature.* New York: Oxford University Press, 1959.

Jones, Howard Mumford and Richard M. Ludwig, *Guide to American Literature and its Backgrounds Since 1890.* 3rd edition Revised and enlarged. Cambridge, Massachusetts: Harvard University Press, 1964.

Killinger, John, *Hemingway and the Dead Gods.* New York: Citadel Press, 1965.

Nyren, Dorothy (ed.), *Library of Literary Criticism.* 3rd edition. New York: Frederick Ungar Publishing Co., 1964.

Sanderson, Stewart, *Ernest Hemingway.* New York: Erie Press, 1961.

Spiller, Robert E. and others (eds.), *Literary History of the United States.* 3rd edition Revised. New York: MacMillan Company, 1963.

Thorp, Willard, *American Writing in the Twentieth Century.* Cambridge, Massachusetts: Harvard University Press, 1963.

Weiss, Irving R. (ed.), *American Authors and Books, 1964 to the Present Day.* New York: Crown Publishers, Inc., 1943.

Westbrook, Max (ed.), *The Modern American Novel: Essays in Criticism.* New York: Random House, 1966.

Young, Phillip, *Ernest Hemingway.* Minneapolis: University of Minnesota Press, 1959.

ERNEST HEMINGWAY

Ernest Hemingway was born in 1899 in Oak Park, Illinois. He served as an ambulance driver for a Red Cross unit in Italy during World War I and was wounded in 1918. He then began a career as a newspaperman and foreign correspondent. His first famous novel was *The Sun Also Rises*, a story about his life in Paris in the 1920's. In 1929 his novel, *A Farewell to Arms*, was even more successful. *For Whom the Bell Tolls*, based on his experiences as a reporter during the Spanish Civil War, was published in 1940. He received the Pulitzer Prize for *The Old Man and the Sea* in 1953 and the Nobel Prize for literature the following year. *A Moveable Feast*, a reminiscence of his early years in Paris, was published posthumously in 1964.

"Papa," as Hemingway was fondly referred to, achieved something of a hero's status in his lifetime. His world travels were covered by the popular magazines of the time, and he was often photographed with the animals he had shot. He worked hard and played hard, as did other popular authors who were his friends, such as F. Scott Fitzgerald. He became a spokesman for the "lost generation"—the generation of people who came of age during the time between the two world wars.

While outwardly he appeared to be a tough, practical man who enjoyed fishing and hunting, his writing clearly reveals a sensitive, compassionate side. The characters in his novels generally conform to a particular code of philosophy and behavior; they face their battles with courage, their pain with endurance. Hemingway himself is often compared with his character Santiago in *The Old Man and the Sea*. But while he believed that "in life one must endure," he himself was ultimately unable to endure his physical and emotional pain. In 1961 he took his own life at his home in Ketchum, Idaho.

Although Hemingway's writing is often criticized, his economical writing style sparkled with brilliance. He was a master in the use of short sentences and simple vocabulary, yet capable of communicating emotion in every sentence. Many authors have tried to imitate his writing style. On the other hand, Hemingway is most often criticized for his portrayal of female characters, who are often unrealistic, domineering, or overly submissive women.

Bibliography

Contemporary Authors, Vol. 77-80. Detroit: Gale Research Co., 1979.

Date _____   Name _____

(AUTHOR PROFILE)

Some of the answers to the following questions may be found in the biography on the preceding page. For other information, check your library.

AUTHOR'S NAME :   *Ernest Hemingway*

1. What has this author written?_____

_____

2. Date of birth _____ Date of death _____

3. What does/did this author look like? _____

_____

_____

4. Where did this author grow up?_____

5. Did this author have any particular difficulties in his life? What were they?

_____

_____

6. What kinds of things does/did this author like to write about most? _____

_____

7. What kind of education does/did this author have? _____

8. What kinds of jobs did this author hold?_____

9. What did you find to be particularly interesting when reading about this author's life?

_____

_____

10. If you could talk to this author in person, what would you like to ask him?

_____

Date _____ Name _____

WORD STUDY

Define the underlined words:

1. "And afterwards it all belongs to you, the good and the bad, the <u>ecstasy</u>, the remorse and sorrow, the people and the places, and how the weather was."

_____

2. The main characters in Hemingway's true but fictional world are <u>individualists</u>.

_____

3. They live by their own code, supported by their own strength of <u>will</u>.

_____

4. And they are often called upon by their code to show courage and <u>endurance</u>, alone against a reality designed to defeat them.

_____

5. He is, first of all, an old man, his skin weathered, his frame <u>gaunt</u>.

_____

6. This time he goes beyond where most of the village fishermen dare to go in their small <u>skiffs</u>.

_____

7. In the boat are <u>reserve</u> coils of line—enough to give a big fish more than 1800 feet, if necessary.

_____

8. He has come to regard the fish as a brother, the two of them linked together in a necessary <u>ritual</u> of death.

_____

9. The fish is the <u>nobler</u> of the two, he admits.

_____

10. Santiago finds enough strength to drive in the <u>harpoon</u>.

_____

Date _____ Name _____

(ANTICIPATION GUIDE)

for the novel *The Old Man and the Sea*

The numbered questions can be answered from reading the synopsis for the novel. Express your own thoughts when answering the questions that are marked with a ⟹.

1. What kind of fish does Santiago catch? _____

    ⟹How big do you imagine this fish to be? _____

_____

2. What are the characteristics of the Hemingway Code? _____

_____

    ⟹Describe a time when you had to be particularly brave. _____

_____

_____

3. What does Santiago dream about in his sleep?_____

_____

    ⟹How do you think these dreams might be significant to the story? _____

_____

_____

4. Santiago comes to regard the fish as his _____

    ⟹Do you think Santiago should kill the fish? Why or why not? _____

_____

_____

5. After he kills the fish, what does Santiago do?_____

_____

    ⟹What do you think will happen to Santiago on his way back to shore?

_____

_____

THE OLD MAN AND THE SEA
Word Search

Using the clues below, find the answers hidden in the puzzle and circle them. They may be printed horizontally, vertically, diagonally, or backward. All of the words are associated with the novel in some way.

```
Y D W S P E O Q C W A H N J M G T W O C
G K L N B C S K T B D B A O N D E F G J
K K J O H S T W T R Z N X X O Q R S X I
Q D W I D T S E A X K W N I I P G T V W
A Q G L G A D K O T H I P G N E R T F D
V H U B U C K O I C F H G K D R H A E D
R H L R O Y E V F J W P C I N E H H U
E R F E K R E L H R F F K A V E O F W O
S L S Z L W F L K Y R S E F I S L N W W
E P T E A D H I W X E N F X D T T M O X
R F R W Y M G W C J D C T I U H C P H R
V I E L X A G J Y U X P N G A E O O I R
E S A J U U O O R F S G R S L M N G H H
B H M N R T P A H K F K E P I I V A U M
S E T Z N P N N Z W V S L X S N S I E X
T R Z P H C I F K J G E B Z T G U T E P
O M F K E M A R L I N Y O X S W I N X E
W A E Y L X L A U T I R N F O A U A O V
O N D E O D F R U F P E I L L Y Z S X Y
Q M E P C D O S B A P D Z N Z S E Q W K
```

1. great joy
2. the old man's occupation
3. a long, barbed spear
4. the fish
5. a solemn ceremony
6. determination
7. power to withstand stress or suffering
8. thin and haggard-looking

9. people who live according to their own rules, not society's
10. better
11. the old man's name
12. author of *The Old Man and the Sea* (two words)
13. mighty ocean current (two words)
14. what the old man dreams about
15. extra
16. small boats

Date _____ Name _____

QUESTIONS FOR STUDY AND DISCUSSION

for the novel *The Old Man and the Sea*

Literal Level

1. Describe the marlin.

_____

_____

_____

2. What happens after Santiago manages to lash the marlin to the skiff?

_____

_____

_____

3. Why does Santiago think he failed to bring in the fish?

_____

_____

_____

4. Cite passages in the novel that indicate Santiago is a skillful fisherman.

_____

_____

_____

5. What kind of relationship do Santiago and the boy, Manolin, have?

_____

_____

_____

QUESTIONS FOR STUDY AND DISCUSSION

for the novel *The Old Man and the Sea*

Interpretive Level

1. What do the lions symbolize?

_____

_____

_____

_____

2. Why do you think Santiago talks to himself and addresses parts of his body as if they were individual personalities?

_____

_____

_____

_____

3. Do you think the novel has a hopeful ending or one of despair? Explain.

_____

_____

_____

_____

Date _____ Name _____

(QUESTIONS FOR STUDY AND DISCUSSION)

for the novel *The Old Man and the Sea*

Critical Level

1. Do you judge the old man to be a religious person? Why or why not?

_____

_____

_____

_____

_____

2. Discuss the symbolic imagery Hemingway uses to describe the old man's suffering when the second and third sharks appear. Do you think the symbolism is effective? Explain.

_____

_____

_____

_____

_____

3. List examples from your own background or other stories you have read about people who have failed to achieve an important goal. What similarities or differences can you find?

_____

_____

_____

_____

_____

ACTIVITIES

for the novel *The Old Man and the Sea*

♣ Prepare a report on fishing in the Gulf Stream. Focus on the individual fishermen rather than the commercial companies. Discuss the hardships and hazards involved in this occupation. Try to find pictures to accompany your report.

♣ Discuss or report on the following topics:
- The tragedy of old age
- The definition of manliness
- The necessity of killing
- Pride and humility
- The meaning of victory and defeat

♣ Imagine you are Manolin, and explain how you feel about Santiago.

♣ Using your own personal experience, write a short story about someone who fails to achieve an important goal.

♣ Make a bulletin board display of photographs of Hemingway taken at various periods in his life.

♣ Considering that *The Old Man and the Sea* was the last novel published before Hemingway's suicide, discuss the following questions:
- Why do you think Hemingway committed suicide?
- Was his suicide consistent with his philosophy as revealed in *The Old Man and the Sea*?

♣ Compare *The Old Man and the Sea* with Hemingway's earlier novels, *A Farewell to Arms* and *For Whom the Bell Tolls*. Discuss ways that the characters of Frederic Henry and Robert Jordan are similar to Hemingway. Does the Hemingway Code apply to them as well as Santiago?

Date _____ Name _____

(VOCABULARY)

from the novel *The Old Man and the Sea*
★ ★

Define the underlined word in each sentence.

1. The brown blotches of the <u>benevolent</u> skin cancer the sun brings from its reflection on the tropic sea were on the old man's cheeks.

_____

2. But, he thought, I keep the lines with <u>precision</u>.

_____

3. The old man was happy to see so much <u>plankton</u> because it meant fish.

_____

4. The tiny fish were <u>immune</u> to the man-of-war's poison.

_____

5. The old man had no <u>mysticism</u> about turtles.

_____

6. The position actually was only somewhat less <u>intolerable</u>.

_____

7. When once, through my <u>treachery</u>, it had been necessary to make a choice, the old man thought.

_____

8. There was plenty of line still and now the fish had to pull the <u>friction</u> of all the new line through the water.

_____

9. The old man did not like to look at the fish anymore since it had been <u>mutilated</u>.

_____

10. The lights of the city were only <u>perceptible</u> before the moon rose.

_____

from the novel *The Old Man and the Sea*
* *

Define the underlined word in each sentence.

11. "I do not like for him to waken me. It is as though I were <u>inferior</u>"

_____

12. As Santiago watched, the bird dipped again slanting his wings for the dive and then swinging them wildly and <u>ineffectively</u>.

_____

13. Nothing showed on the surface of the water but the <u>gelatinous</u> bladder of a Portuguese man-of-war.

_____

14. The old man had a friendly <u>contempt</u> for the huge loggerheads.

_____

15. The <u>myriad</u> flecks of the plankton were annulled now by the high sun.

_____

16. The <u>lavender</u> wings, that were his pectoral fins, spread wide.

_____

17. The blood <u>coagulated</u> before it reached the old man's chin.

_____

18. It is better to be light-headed than to lose your strength from <u>nausea</u>.

_____

19. The old man drove the blade between the <u>vertebrae</u> and the brain.

_____

20. Santiago knew he was beaten now and without <u>remedy</u>.

_____

Date _____ Name _____

THE OLD MAN AND THE SEA CROSSWORD PUZZLE

Use what you have learned from the novel to complete the puzzle. Many of the words are taken from the vocabulary study.

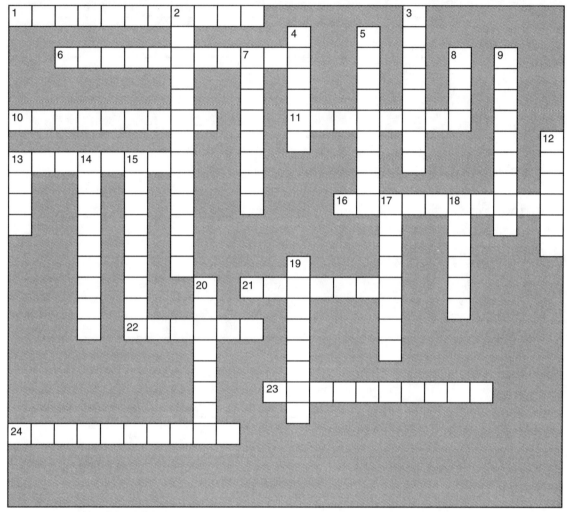

ACROSS

1. able to be seen
6. unable to be endured
10. maimed
11. Santiago believes a man can be _____ but not destroyed
13. scorn
16. resembling jelly
21. Santiago's young friend
22. a great number
23. clotted
24. not harmful

DOWN

2. unsuccessfully
3. tiny marine organisms
4. cure
5. spinal column
7. the animals of the sea are this to Santiago
8. flying visitor to Santiago's skiff
9. exactness
12. a sick feeling in the stomach
13. Santiago's homeland
14. betrayal
15. spiritual feeling
17. pale purple
18. not susceptible
19. lower in quality
20. resistance

Date _____ Name _____

PART I: VOCABULARY (20 points)
Write the definition of the word in the space next to it.

1. nausea _____

2. precision _____

3. perceptible _____

4. lavender _____

5. inferior _____

6. benevolent _____

7. plankton _____

8. myriad _____

9. remedy _____

10. coagulated _____

11. friction _____

12. mysticism _____

13. ineffectively _____

14. mutilated _____

15. vertebrae _____

16. immune _____

17. treachery _____

18. gelatinous _____

19. intolerable _____

20. contempt _____

PART II: TRUE OR FALSE (10 points)

In the space provided, write *true* if the statement is completely true, or write *false* if any part of the statement is false.

_____ 1. After 84 days without catching a fish, Santiago tells Manolin that he has lost his confidence.

_____ 2. The marlin swallows the hook immediately upon taking the bait.

_____ 3. Santiago thinks of the porpoises and flying fish as his brothers.

_____ 4. The marlin is the biggest fish Santiago has ever caught.

_____ 5. Santiago tries to haul the carcass of the great fish onto his skiff so that the sharks will be unable to get to it.

_____ 6. Once hooked, the marlin pulls the boat farther out to sea.

_____ 7. After struggling with the marlin Santiago knows that he is still as strong as he was in his youth.

_____ 8. Even though Santiago loves the marlin, he is determined to kill it.

_____ 9. Santiago reaches a point in his struggle with the fish where he doesn't care if he kills the fish or the fish kills him.

_____ 10. Santiago is determined to fight the sharks until he dies.

PART III: MULTIPLE CHOICE (30 points)

Decide which is the best response for each of the following sentences. Write the letter of your choice in the space provided.

_____ 1. The old man often dreams about:
  (a) lions on the beach
  (b) storms at sea
  (c) catching great fish
  (d) Manolin

_____ 2. When Santiago gets a cramp in his hand he:
  (a) doesn't notice
  (b) screams in pain
  (c) speaks to it
  (d) gives up and goes home

_____ 3. The struggle with the great fish proves to Santiago that he:
  (a) can endure
  (b) is nobler than the fish
  (c) can conquer anything in the sea
  (d) is as strong as he was in his youth

_____ 4. Toward the end of his struggle with the fish, Santiago:
  (a) yells at the fish for causing him so much pain
  (b) no longer cares who kills whom
  (c) says a hundred Our Fathers and a hundred Hail Mary's
  (d) gives up and goes home

_____ 5. The old man considers the sea to be:
  (a) masculine
  (b) feminine
  (c) his enemy
  (d) his best friend

_____ 6. Santiago believes that a man can be:
  (a) immortal
  (b) easily beaten
  (c) defeated but not destroyed
  (d) destroyed but not defeated.

_____ 7. The style of the novel is best described as:
  (a) elaborately ornamental
  (b) sarcastic
  (c) starkly simple
  (d) heavily verbose

_____ 8. Santiago feels sharks are:
  (a) hateful because they are scavengers as well as killers
  (b) his brothers
  (c) simply part of nature
  (d) nobler than the marlin

_____ 9. The boy does not go out to sea with the old man because:
  (a) the old man doesn't like him hanging around
  (b) the boy's parents order him to go out with another fisherman
  (c) the boy has learned all that Santiago can teach him
  (d) the old man no longer needs his help

_____ 10. The old man knows that humility:
  (a) is a sin
  (b) is an excuse for weak men
  (c) carries no loss of true pride
  (d) can only be obtained by submitting to God's will

_____ 11. Santiago feels all but one of the following toward the great fish:
  (a) love
  (b) respect
  (c) hate
  (d) the desire to kill it

_____ 12. Santiago feels that killing the marlin is the same as killing:
   (a) any enemy
   (b) his brother
   (c) his best friend
   (d) a child of God

_____ 13. Santiago finally kills the marlin by:
   (a) harpooning it
   (b) tying his knife to an oar and stabbing it
   (c) clubbing it with an oar
   (d) shooting it with his rifle

_____ 14. The old man does not like to look at the marlin after it is:
   (a) dead
   (b) lashed to the boat
   (c) mutilated
   (d) cut up into fish steaks

_____ 15. Santiago believes the major cause of his failure is:
   (a) not having a gun in the boat
   (b) going out too far
   (c) not taking the boy along
   (d) not taking enough food to keep his strength up

PART IV: ESSAY (40 points)

Answer <u>two</u> of the following essay questions.

1. Discuss whether, in your opinion, Santiago is a success or a failure.

2. How is the relationship between Santiago and Manolin important to the story?

3. What is the philosophy about growing old and dying that Hemingway expresses in this novel?

4. Describe and explain the significance of the symbolism in *The Old Man and the Sea*.

ANSWER KEY

Answers to Word Study (page 48)
1. ecstasy: great joy
2. individualists: people who live according to their own rules, not society's
3. will: determination
4. endurance: power to withstand stress or suffering
5. gaunt: thin and haggard-looking
6. skiffs: small boats
7. reserve: extra
8. ritual: a solemn ceremony
9. nobler: better
10. harpoon: a long, barbed spear

Answers to Anticipation Guide (page 49)
1. marlin
2. courage and endurance amid constant pain, past the point when the body seemingly has no strength left but the strength of the spirit inside
3. lions playing on the beach in Africa
4. brother
5. lashes the fish to the boat, raises the sail, and sails for land

Answers to Word Search (page 50)
1. ECSTACY
2. FISHERMAN
3. HARPOON
4. MARLIN
5. RITUAL
6. WILL
7. ENDURANCE
8. GAUNT
9. INDIVIDUALISTS
10. NOBLER
11. SANTIAGO
12. ERNEST HEMINGWAY
13. GULF STREAM
14. LIONS
15. RESERVE
16. SKIFFS

Answers to Questions for Study and Discussion
Literal Level (page 51)
1. It is over 1500 lbs. and larger than the old man's boat; purple and silver; the tail and stripes are pale violet; stripes are wider than a man's spread hand; eye looks detached as the mirrors in a periscope or as a saint in a procession.

2. Sharks attack, attracted by the scent of the marlin's blood. Santiago beats them off, but there are too many of them and he can't prevent them from eating the marlin.

3. Because he went out too far.

4. He knows he must tire the fish and prevent him from diving; he knows if the fish jumps it will fill the air sacks along its backbone with air which will keep him from diving deep; he knows not to tie the line to the boat, but rather to control the tension in the line with his body, in order to keep the line from breaking. Students may find many other passages indicating Santiago's great skill as a fisherman.

5. There is clearly a lot of love between the old man and the boy. Santiago had taught Manolin how to fish; Manolin shows his love by taking care of Santiago and speaking to him respectfully. Santiago often thinks of the boy during his long ordeal with the fish. In the end it is the boy who comforts Santiago after his failure to bring in the great fish.

Interpretive Level (page 52)
1. The lions may symbolize Santiago's youthful spirit, in spite of his age and physical weakness. They may also symbolize the nobility in the old man. Students may have other acceptable interpretations.

2. Possibly Santiago talks to his body simply because he is a lonely old man. Or it may be his attempt to impose his will upon an aged body that has been pushed beyond endurance. Physically, he would like to give up, but his will commands his body to go on.

3. Answers will vary.

Critical Level (page 53)
1. Santiago observes the outward forms of Catholicism, but is evidently not deeply committed to traditional Christianity. On the other hand, his love for the fish as his brother, and his regard for the fish as something nobler than himself indicate a more deeply spiritual sense. Students may cite other references that back up their judgment.

2. The passage is an obvious allusion to the crucifixion of Christ. Students' opinions may vary as to whether or not it is effective.

ANSWER KEY

3. Answers will vary.

Answers to Crossword Puzzle (page 57)

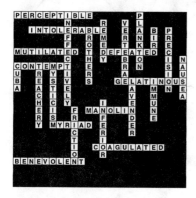

Answers to Test
PART I: VOCABULARY (page 58)

1. nausea
   (a sick feeling in the stomach)
2. precision
   (exactness)
3. perceptible
   (able to be seen)
4. lavender
   (pale purple)
5. inferior
   (lower in quality)
6. benevolent
   (not harmful)
7. plankton
   (tiny marine organisms)
8. myriad
   (a great number)
9. remedy
   (cure)
10. coagulated
    (clotted)
11. friction
    (resistance)
12. mysticism
    (spiritual feeling)
13. ineffectively
    (unsuccessfully)
14. mutilated
    (maimed)
15. vertebrae
    (spinal column)
16. immune
    (not susceptible)
17. treachery
    (betrayal)
18. gelatinous
    (resembling jelly)
19. intolerable
    (unable to be endured)
20. contempt
    (scorn)

PART II: TRUE OR FALSE (page 59)

1. false
2. false
3. true
4. true
5. false
6. true
7. false
8. true
9. true
10. true

PART III: MULTIPLE CHOICE (pages 59-61)

1. A
2. C
3. A
4. B
5. B
6. C
7. C
8. A
9. B
10. C
11. C
12. B
13. A
14. C
15. B

PART IV: ESSAY (page 61)
Answers will vary.

THE CALL OF THE WILD

by Jack London

SYNOPSIS

He is four years old in the autumn of 1897. Not so large as his Saint Bernard father, but much larger than his shepherd mother, and larger than most wolves. His name is Buck, and he lives what in human terms would be called the "life of a country gentleman" on Judge Miller's California estate. As the judge's favorite dog, he has the run of the whole place.

Buck is really everybody's favorite dog. He goes hunting with the judge's sons and gives the little grandsons rides on his back. Whenever someone plunges into the swimming tank on a warm California afternoon, Buck plunges in along with them. That is Buck's life, the only life he has known.

But now that life is about to change—drastically. One of the gardener's helpers needs money, and the judge's dog, Buck, is an easy way to get it. Nobody else at Judge Miller's will know what happened to Buck. He will just be gone, like so many other big, thick-haired dogs up and down the West Coast of the United States.

Dogs like this are extremely valuable in the autumn of 1897. Gold was discovered the year before on Klondike Creek, near the Alaskan-Canadian border. The rush is on, and another winter is coming. Sled dogs—thousands of them—will be needed.

So Buck begins a long journey to a place from which he will never return. A journey north, a journey away from civilization. And also a journey in time, backward, far back, to an almost—but not quite—forgotten ancestral past.

Jack London is the author of *The Call of the Wild.* In the words of one critic, "The greatest story he wrote was the story he lived." Certainly his life had as much adventure as any of his stories. At 17, he signed on a seal-hunting vessel as an able-bodied seaman, traveling across the Pacific to the coast of Siberia. Back in the states, he became a hobo for awhile, was arrested for vagrancy, and served a term in jail. He had decided early that he wanted to be a writer. After his release from jail, he went back to school, spending a semester at the University of California. He might have completed college, but he was running out of money.

In 1897, at age 21, he went north, along with thousands of others, to where gold had been struck on Klondike Creek in Canada's Yukon Territory. The ship landed the would-be miners near Skagway, Alaska. To reach the Klondike region, London and the others first had to climb the steep Chilkoot Pass with packs weighing over 100 pounds. In London's pack,

64

together with grub, were books like Darwin's *Origin of Species* and Milton's *Paradise Lost.*

Jack London mined no gold in the Klondike; he didn't even really try. But as a writer, he found a wealth of material which his talent would later turn into gold. He "mined" this material for all it was worth. In the Yukon, where the struggle for survival was clear-cut and unrefined, London found exactly the right setting for many of the themes that excited him as a young writer, like the theme of the super man, or, as in *The Call of the Wild,* super dog. London took this idea from the German philosopher Fredric Neitzsche, who glorified power and despised weakness. London, in his own philosophy, mixed the ideas of Neitzsche with the socialist ideas of Karl Marx and added the popular interpretation of Darwin's "survival of the fittest." The result, said one critic, was "mental indigestion."

Yet, as a basis for fiction, London's philosophical mixture often worked well, particularly in *The Call of the Wild.* Here the author's philosophical ideas stay in the background. They motivate a forceful, action-filled narrative that takes the main character away from civilized ease, through cruel hardships and violent brutality, to a final state of primitive splendor.

The main character happens to be a dog—but a symbolic dog, which the author endows with the psychology and feelings of a human being. Buck is a dog with whom the reader can identify. Buck learns quickly what the author calls the "law of club and fang," for what in human terms used to be called the "law of hard knocks"—something that London himself, no doubt, learned early.

The first lesson for Buck—who was in a rage after having been kidnapped and put on a train to Seattle—is that a man with a club must be respected and obeyed. After charging more than a dozen times at the man with the club, and each time being smashed to the ground, Buck knows and accepts that he is beaten—not broken, but for now, beaten.

Buck is purchased in Seattle by two French-Canadians. The Canadian government employs them to carry dispatches by dog team between the coast and the mining town of Dawson. Buck's new owners take him and three other dogs north from Seattle by ship. They land in southern Alaska, near Skagway, where London himself landed. The two French-Canadians immediately set about assembling a full team. Buck, meanwhile, has his first experience with something called snow. He also learns another lesson about the law of club and fang; luckily for him, not directly. The victim is Curly, a big Newfoundland, also from the south. Curly, meaning to be friendly, is savagely attacked by an Eskimo dog, or Husky. The other Huskies quickly form a circle around the two and wait. It soon becomes obvious that the Newfoundland, though big, is no match for the fight-experienced Husky. And once down, even for a moment, no quarter is given. The watching Huskies quickly close in and tear the fallen dog to pieces. Buck sees it happen, and the lesson is learned. He will never let it happen to him.

The time is coming when Buck will be put to the test against a white Husky named Spitz. The two French-Canadians have chosen Spitz to be the leader of the team. But already a rivalry—soon to be a deadly rivalry—is growing between Spitz and Buck. Nevertheless, Buck still has a lot to learn. Most importantly, he has to learn how to be a sled dog, how to pull in harness as part of a team—something for which his life in California in no way prepared him. Neither did his California life prepare him for something as ordinary, to a sled dog, as digging a warm place to sleep under the snow. He is used to sleeping indoors, which is definitely not to be the case here. Buck is a tenderfoot, like many of the dogs and most of the men caught up in the Klondike gold rush. Some adapt to the Northland;

some perish. Buck adapts. He is a natural winner, no matter what the circumstances. And by the time the team is making the return run from Dawson to the coast, Buck has vanquished Spitz and is leading the team himself—very much like the author, who always strove to be tops at whatever he did.

But something else is happening to Buck. Sometimes after a day's work, when he is crouching near the fire, staring into the flames, it seems to be another fire, long ago, with another kind of man for his master. As a sled dog in the here-and-now, Buck is destined to have more than one kind of master, for at the end of each run the team changes owners–until the worst happens.

Buck and his teammates are bought by a trio of inexperienced prospectors: two men and a woman. Pulling an overloaded sled, whipped and clubbed without mercy, starving, Buck finally decides he has had enough. He senses, too, that something is wrong with the trail. Even though he is being clubbed to death, he refuses to go on. Buck is saved by a prospector, John Thornton, who has been watching the tragic proceedings from his camp by a frozen river. Thornton, after knocking down Buck's tormentor, cuts the dog loose from his traces. The three greenhorns go on. They have been warned not to go any farther, since spring is coming and the ice is beginning to melt on the river—something which Buck sensed. Now Buck and Thornton watch as the trail drops out and all are lost beneath the ice.

Buck has found a new master, one that he can not only serve, but love. And with rest and good treatment, the dog regains his former strength. He has never been happier. Yet, the old visions of a distant past come more frequently now. And back even further, there is the call of a still more distant time—a call which Buck feels an urge to answer. How much longer will even the love of a good master be able to hold him?

Do you want to know more about Buck and his adventures? Read the rest of the novel!

BIBLIOGRAPHY

Franchere, Ruth, *Jack London: The Pursuit of a Dream*. New York: Thomas Y. Crowell, 1962.

Heiney, Donald, *Recent American Literature,* Vol. 4. Woodbury, New York: Barron's Educational Series, Inc., 1959.

Knight, Grant C., *The Strenuous Age in American Literature*. Raleigh, North Carolina: University of North Carolina Press, 1954.

Nyren, Dorothy (ed.), *Library of Literary Criticism, Modern American Literature*. New York: Frederick Ungar Publishing Co., 1964.

O'Connor, Richard, *Jack London, A Biography*. Boston: Little, Brown and Co., 1964.

Quinn, Arthur H., *Literature of the American People, An Historical and Critical Survey*. New York: Appleton-Century-Crofts, Inc., 1951.

Stone, Irving, *Jack London, Sailor on Horseback*. New York: Pocket Books, 1964.

Van Doren, Mark, *The American Novel, 1789-1939*. New York: MacMillan, 1940.

Wagenknecht, Edward, *Cavalcade of the American Novel*. New York: Holt, Rinehart & Winston, 1952.

JACK LONDON

Jack London was born in San Francisco in 1876 and grew up in the Oakland, California area. His family was poor and moved often. Rejected by his natural father, he also did not receive much attention or affection from his mother or stepfather. Feeling lonely and

insecure, he spent many hours in the Oakland Public Library, where he found solace and comfort in books. His difficult childhood eventually led him into a number of different jobs before the age of twenty-three, including sailor, gold hunter in Alaska, longshoreman, and war correspondent during the Russo-Japanese War. He even lived the life of a hobo for awhile, riding underneath the cars of freight trains. In New York he was arrested for vagrancy and spent a month in the Erie County Penitentiary. At this point he became a socialist and returned to Oakland to prepare for college. He entered the University of California, but left after one semester. In 1897 he joined the Yukon gold rush. Even while he was camping in the Klondike, he continued to read widely. His favorite novel was *Moby Dick* by Herman Melville.

The experience London gained from his unconventional lifestyle and travels in the Klondike gave him the background from which to write several powerful novels and short stories, including *The Call of the Wild* (1903) and *White Fang* (1906). *The Call of the Wild* tells the story of a civilized dog who reverts to his primitive heritage, while *White Fang* recounts the opposite story about a wild dog who becomes civilized. Other important novels by Jack London include *The Sea-Wolf* and *Martin Eden*.

London was one of America's most famous authors, and his private life became public news. He lived lavishly, but beyond his means. The mansion he built in the Sonoma Valley of California burned just as it was being completed. A daughter died just a few days after her birth. He drank heavily and was occasionally involved in barroom brawls. The hard drinking ultimately affected his health, and he also suffered from acute rheumatism. He died in 1916 at the age of 41 after taking an overdose of morphine. It is not known whether he committed suicide or died accidentally.

Bibiliography
Contemporary Authors, Vol. 119. Detroit: Gale Research Co., 1987.

Date _____ Name _____

AUTHOR PROFILE

Some of the answers to the following questions may be found in the biography on the preceding page. For other information, check your library.

AUTHOR'S NAME :   *Jack London*

1. What has this author written?_____

_____

2. Date of birth _____ Date of death _____

3. What does/did this author look like? _____

_____

4. Where did this author grow up?_____

5. Did this author have any particular difficulties in his life? What were they?

_____

_____

6. What kinds of things does/did this author like to write about most? _____

_____

7. What kind of education does/did this author have? _____

8. What kinds of jobs did this author hold? _____

9. What did you find to be particularly interesting when reading about this author's life?

_____

_____

10. If you could talk to this author in person, what would you like to ask him?

_____

Date _____ Name _____

WORD STUDY

Define the underlined words:

1. And also a journey in time, backward, far back, to an almost—but not quite—forgotten <u>ancestral</u> past.

_____

2. Back in the states, he became a hobo for awhile, was arrested for <u>vagrancy</u>, and served a term in jail.

_____

3. In London's pack, together with <u>grub</u>, were books like Darwin's *Origin of Species* and Milton's *Paradise Lost*.

_____

4. London, in his own <u>philosophy</u>, mixed the ideas of Neitzsche with the socialist ideas of Karl Marx . . .

_____

5. They motivate a forceful, action-filled narrative that takes the main character away from civilized ease . . . to a final state of <u>primitive</u> splendor.

_____

6. The main character happens to be a dog—but a symbolic dog, which the author <u>endows</u> with the psychology and feelings of a human being.

_____

7. But already a <u>rivalry</u>—soon to be a deadly rivalry—is growing between Spitz and Buck.

_____

8. Buck is a <u>tenderfoot</u>, like many of the dogs and most of the men caught up in the Klondike gold rush.

_____

9. And by the time the team is making the return run from Dawson to the coast, Buck has <u>vanquished</u> Spitz and is leading the team himself . . .

_____

10. Buck is saved by a <u>prospector</u>, John Thornton, who has been watching the tragic proceedings from his camp by a frozen river.

_____

Date _____ Name _____

(ANTICIPATION GUIDE)

for the novel *The Call of the Wild*

The numbered questions can be answered from reading the synopsis for the novel. Express your own thoughts when answering the questions that are marked with a ⟹.

1. Who is responsible for taking Buck away from his California home? _____

_____

⟹Do you think Buck is aware of the danger that lies before him? Explain.

_____

_____

2. For what crime was the author, Jack London, arrested and sent to jail? _____

_____

⟹Do you think this experience might have influenced his writing? Why or why not?

_____

_____

3. What is the law that Buck learns quickly when he becomes a sled dog? _____

_____

⟹What are some ways that humans learn things through the law of hard knocks?

_____

_____

4. What happens to the three prospectors and the team after John Thornton rescues Buck?

_____

_____

⟹Do you think Buck and John Thornton will live"happily ever after"? Why or why not?

_____

5. What are the visions that Buck has with increasing frequency?_____

_____

⟹What do you think the visions represent? _____

_____

Date _____   Name _____

THE CALL OF THE WILD
Word Search

Using the clues below, find the answers hidden in the puzzle and circle them. They may be printed horizontally, vertically, diagonally, or backward. All of the words are associated with the novel in some way.

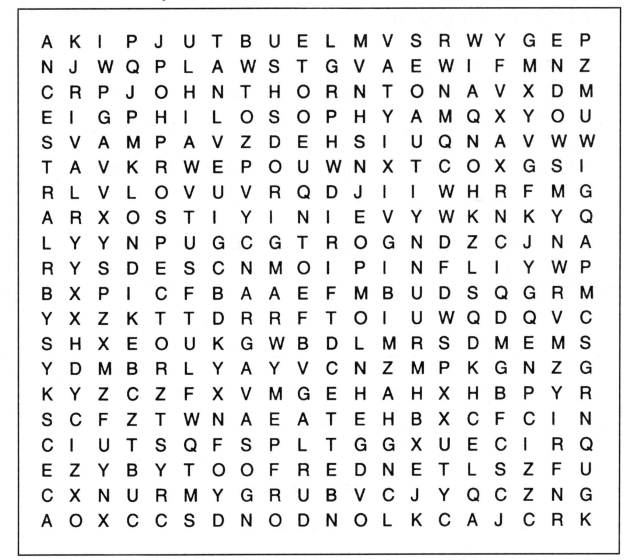

```
A  K  I  P  J  U  T  B  U  E  L  M  V  S  R  W  Y  G  E  P
N  J  W  Q  P  L  A  W  S  T  G  V  A  E  W  I  F  M  N  Z
C  R  P  J  O  H  N  T  H  O  R  N  T  O  N  A  V  X  D  M
E  I  G  P  H  I  L  O  S  O  P  H  Y  A  M  Q  X  Y  O  U
S  V  A  M  P  A  V  Z  D  E  H  S  I  U  Q  N  A  V  W  W
T  A  V  K  R  W  E  P  O  U  W  N  X  T  C  O  X  G  S  I
R  L  V  L  O  U  V  R  Q  D  J  I  I  W  H  R  F  M  G
A  R  X  O  S  T  I  Y  I  N  I  E  V  Y  W  K  N  K  Y  Q
L  Y  Y  N  P  U  G  C  G  T  R  O  G  N  D  Z  C  J  N  A
R  Y  S  D  E  S  C  N  M  O  I  P  I  N  F  L  I  Y  W  P
B  X  P  I  C  F  B  A  A  E  F  M  B  U  D  S  Q  G  R  M
Y  X  Z  K  T  T  D  R  R  F  T  O  I  U  W  Q  D  Q  V  C
S  H  X  E  O  U  K  G  W  B  D  L  M  R  S  D  M  E  M  S
Y  D  M  B  R  L  Y  A  Y  V  C  N  Z  M  P  K  G  N  Z  G
K  Y  Z  C  Z  F  X  V  M  G  E  H  A  H  X  H  B  P  Y  R
S  C  F  Z  T  W  N  A  E  A  T  E  H  B  X  C  F  C  I  N
C  I  U  T  S  Q  F  S  P  L  T  G  G  X  U  E  C  I  R  Q
E  Z  Y  B  Y  T  O  O  F  R  E  D  N  E  T  L  S  Z  F  U
C  X  N  U  R  M  Y  G  R  U  B  V  C  J  Y  Q  C  Z  N  G
A  O  X  C  C  S  D  N  O  D  N  O  L  K  C  A  J  C  R  K
```

1. pertaining to relatives from the past
2. furnishes
3. the man who rescues the dog from cruel masters (two words)
4. original
5. one who is new to something
6. the dog's name
7. food
8. the creek where gold was discovered

9. one who searches for valuable minerals
10. wandering, homeless
11. the law that the dog must learn (three words)
12. author of *The Call of the Wild* (two words)
13. beliefs about knowledge, thought, conduct, and nature
14. competition
15. conquered

Date _____ Name _____

QUESTIONS FOR STUDY AND DISCUSSION

for the novel *The Call of the Wild*

Literal Level

1. What is the law of club and fang?

_____

_____

_____

_____

_____

2. List each of Buck's masters and the environment he lives in with them.

_____

_____

_____

_____

_____

3. What incidents from the novel show that Buck is a superb fighting animal?

_____

_____

_____

_____

_____

Date _____ Name _____

QUESTIONS FOR STUDY AND DISCUSSION

for the novel *The Call of the Wild*

Interpretive Level

1. Who is the master that Buck comes to love deeply? In what ways does Buck demonstrate his great love?

_____

_____

_____

_____

_____

_____

2. Explain what happens to Hal, Charles, and Mercedes. Do they deserve their fate? Why or why not?

_____

_____

_____

_____

_____

_____

Date _____ Name _____

(QUESTIONS FOR STUDY AND DISCUSSION)

for the novel *The Call of the Wild*

<u>Critical Level</u>

1. Describe the character of John Thornton. Is it important to the plot that he die? Why or why not? Do you think he deserved to be murdered? Explain.

_____

_____

_____

_____

_____

2. What is the plot structure of *The Call of the Wild*? Is it effective? Why or why not?

_____

_____

_____

_____

3. What are some of the themes in *The Call of the Wild*? Explain.

_____

_____

_____

_____

_____

ACTIVITIES

for the novel *The Call of the Wild*

♣ Discuss or write an essay on the following topics:
- Survival of the Fittest
- The Lure of Gold
- Animal and Human Loyalty

♣ Using your own experiences and observations, write a short story about an animal. It can be fiction or non-fiction.

♣ Debate the following question:

Is the will to dominate others a natural human drive?

♣ Design a bulletin board display including drawings and photographs of the Klondike Gold Rush, dog teams, mining camps, and the frontier towns of Dawson and Skagway. You might also include drawings of scenes from the novel.

♣ Compare and contrast *The Call of the Wild* with Jack London's *White Fang* or with Sheila Burnford's *The Incredible Journey*.

♣ As a class, make a list of qualities necessary for survival in a savage environment and a list of qualities necessary for survival in a civilized society. Discuss any similarities and differences you find.

♣ Research and report on the following topics:
- Klondike Gold Rush
- The Value of Dogs for Transportation in the Arctic
- The Climate of the Yukon Territory

Date _____ Name _____

VOCABULARY

from the novel *The Call of the Wild*

* *

Define the underlined word in each sentence.

1. Buck had merely <u>intimated</u> his displeasure.

_____

2. Perrault and Francois were fair men, calm and <u>impartial</u> in administering justice.

_____

3. Buck's development (or <u>retrogression</u>) was rapid.

_____

4. The <u>insidious</u> revolt led by Buck has destroyed the solidarity of the team.

_____

5. There was no hope for Spitz. Buck was <u>inexorable</u>.

_____

6. Hal's cartridge belt advertised his <u>callowness</u>.

_____

7. As Buck grew stronger Keet and Nig <u>enticed</u> him into all sorts of ridiculous games.

_____

8. O'Brien thumped down a <u>plethoric</u> sack by the side of Matthewson's.

_____

9. Buck and the hairy man were alert and <u>vigilant</u>.

_____

10. Buck killed to eat, not for <u>wantonness</u>.

_____

VOCABULARY

from the novel *The Call of the Wild*

* *

Define the underlined word in each sentence.

11. "Answers to the name of Buck," the man <u>soliloquized</u>.

_____

12. The man's club had beaten into Buck a more <u>fundamental</u> and primitive code.

_____

13. The <u>domesticated</u> generations fell from Buck.

_____

14. Francois swore strange barbarous oaths and stamped the snow in <u>futile</u> rage.

_____

15. Francois was <u>obdurate</u>.

_____

16. In the excess of their own misery, the newcomers were <u>callous</u> to the suffering of their animals.

_____

17. Buck romped through his <u>convalescence</u> and into a new existence.

_____

18. The men were bubbling over in a general <u>incoherent</u> babel.

_____

19. In the end, Buck's <u>pertinacity</u> was rewarded.

_____

20. Forest and stream and air seemed <u>palpitant</u> with the presence of life.

_____

Date _____ Name _____

THE CALL OF THE WILD
CROSSWORD PUZZLE

Use what you have learned from the novel to complete the puzzle. Many of the words are taken from the vocabulary study.

ACROSS

1. recovery
6. basic
7. malicious, immoral
10. watchful
14. survival of the _____
16. immaturity
18. stubborn
20. Buck's ancestors
21. useless
22. unbiased
23. tamed
24. excessively abundant
25. disordered and unconnected

DOWN

2. spoke to oneself
3. tempted
4. unyielding
5. wily or treacherous
8. Alaskan town
9. hinted
11. miners hoped to find it
12. hardened
13. holding firmly to a purpose
15. Buck's canine enemy
17. quivering
19. backward movement or wasteful behavior

Date _____ Name _____

PART I: VOCABULARY (20 points)

Write the definition of the word in the space next to it.

1. plethoric _____

2. fundamental _____

3. impartial _____

4. wantonness _____

5. pertinacity _____

6. soliloquized _____

7. retrogression _____

8. callous _____

9. intimated _____

10. palpitant _____

11. domesticated _____

12. insidious _____

13. callowness _____

14. convalescence _____

15. obdurate _____

16. enticed _____

17. incoherent _____

18. vigilant _____

19. futile _____

20. inexorable _____

PART II: TRUE OR FALSE (10 points)

In the space provided, write *true* if the statement is completely true, or write *false* if any part of the statement is false.

_____ 1. Buck is not hurt or disappointed when Perrault and Francois leave his life forever.

_____ 2. Hal and Charles cannot carry enough food for the fourteen dogs on their team.

_____ 3. After he learns to love John Thornton, Buck no longer hears the call of the wild.

_____ 4. John Thornton is not really interested in searching for gold.

_____ 5. One of the themes of the novel is that the unfit do not deserve to survive.

_____ 6. Manuel sells Buck because he cannot afford to keep him.

_____ 7. Perrault and Francois immediately make Buck the leader of their dog team since he is large and strong.

_____ 8. Hal nearly beats Buck to death because he refuses to cross the White River.

_____ 9. Buck is strong, but not strong enough to pull a sled loaded with half a ton of flour.

_____10. Buck's character is larger than life and more human than canine.

PART III: MULTIPLE CHOICE (30 points)

Decide which is the best response for each of the following sentences. Write the letter of your choice in the space provided.

_____ 1. The law of the club refers to:
    (a) the dominance of man
    (b) survival of the fittest
    (c) rules of the trace and trail
    (d) rules for being a member of a dog team

_____ 2. All of the humans that Buck encounters in the Northland:
    (a) demonstrate their respect for him
    (b) abuse and mistreat him
    (c) love him
    (d) pass out of his life forever

_____ 3. Buck's chief antagonist on the trail is:
      (a) Francois
      (b) Dave
      (c) Spitz
      (d) a wild wolf

_____ 4. The reason that Hal, Charles, and Mercedes fail to survive in the wilderness
      is that they:
      (a) insist on traveling in the winter
      (b) are punished by God for being cruel and greedy
      (c) fail to adapt to their environment
      (d) are overcome by their lust for gold

_____ 5. Buck proves his loyalty to John Thornton by all of the following except:
      (a) trying to jump off a cliff at Thornton's command
      (b) killing Burton
      (c) saving Thornton from drowning in the rapids
      (d) pulling a sled loaded with a thousand pounds of flour

_____ 6. Buck often dreams about:
      (a) the ways of his ancestors
      (b) his California home
      (c) chasing rabbits
      (d) leading a dog team over the wilderness trail

_____ 7. Buck is finally free to respond to the call of the wild when Thornton:
      (a) drives him away
      (b) returns to civilization
      (c) finds gold
      (d) dies

_____ 8. *The Call of the Wild* is primarily a:
      (a) philosophical novel
      (b) naturalistic novel
      (c) romantic and adventurous novel
      (d) purely autobiographical novel

_____ 9. Buck learns the law of the club from:
      (a) the judge
      (b) the man in the red sweater
      (c) Perrault and Francois
      (d) the Scotch half-breed

_____ 10. The law of the fang refers to:
      (a) the dominance of man
      (b) survival of the fittest
      (c) rules of the trace and trail
      (d) rules for being a member of a dog team

_____ 11. Hal, Charles, and Mercedes die:
      (a) of starvation
      (b) in a raging blizzard
      (c) in an Indian attack
      (d) in the waters of the White River

_____ 12. With the money he wins in a bet, Thornton:
   (a) buys land in the Klondike
   (b) finances a gold-prospecting expedition
   (c) establishes a business in Dawson
   (d) becomes a famous explorer of the arctic wilderness

_____ 13. The only thing that brings Buck back from hunting in the wilderness is:
   (a) his love for John Thornton
   (b) a warm place to sleep next to Thornton's campfire
   (c) the call of the wild
   (d) starvation

_____ 14. Buck's character development may be best described as:
   (a) growth toward love and devotion
   (b) retrogression to the primitive
   (c) gradual submission to the law of the club and fang
   (d) transformation into a mindless, savage beast

_____ 15. One of the major themes of *The Call of the Wild* is:
   (a) the strong must protect the weak
   (b) the strong survive and the weak perish
   (c) man dominates his environment
   (d) civilized man is superior to savage animals

PART IV: ESSAY (40 points)
Answer <u>two</u> of the following essay questions.

1. Discuss how Buck learns to adapt to and ultimately dominate his environment.

2. Various animal characters in the novel are endowed with human characteristics. Describe them and explain why you think the author endowed them with these traits.

3. Discuss the effect that the various human characters have on Buck's life.

ANSWER KEY

Answers to Word Study (page 69)
1. ancestral: pertaining to relatives from the past
2. vagrancy: wandering, homeless
3. grub: food
4. philosophy: beliefs about knowledge, thought, conduct, and nature
5. primitive: original
6. endows: furnishes
7. rivalry: competition
8. tenderfoot: one who is new to something
9. vanquished: conquered
10. prospector: one who searches for valuable minerals

Answers to Anticipation Guide (page 70)
1. Manuel, one of the gardener's helpers
2. vagrancy
3. the law of club and fang
4. they fall through the ice on the river and are drowned
5. visions of a distant, ancestral past

Answers to Word Search (page 71)
1. ANCESTRAL
2. ENDOWS
3. JOHN THORNTON
4. PRIMITIVE
5. TENDERFOOT
6. BUCK
7. GRUB
8. KLONDIKE
9. PROSPECTOR
10. VAGRANT
11. CLUB AND FANG
12. JACK LONDON
13. PHILOSOPHY
14. RIVALRY
15. VANQUISHED

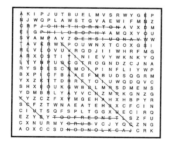

Answers to Questions for Study and Discussion
Literal Level (page 72)
1. The law of the club refers to man's dominance over animals through superior force and brutality. The law of the fang refers to survival of the fittest.

2. Judge Miller: estate in Santa Clara Valley, California; Perrault and Francois: Dyea Beach and the journey to the Northland; Scotch half-breed: mail run between Skagway and Dawson; Charles, Hal, and Mercedes: brutal treatment in the Northland; John Thornton: Buck remains with him until Thornton's death

3. the battle with Spitz; his revenge against the Yeehats. Students will be able to cite many other references to Buck's fighting ability.

Interpretive Level (page &3)
1. John Thornton. Five incidents illustrate Buck's devotion to him:
    (a) Buck's willingness to jump over a cliff on Thornton's command
    (b) His violent attack on Burton, a miner who had hit Thornton
    (c) His heroic rescue of Thornton from the churning river
    (d) His winning of $1000 for Thornton by pulling a thousand pounds
    (e) He avenges John's murder by attacking the Yeehat Indians

2. Hal, Charles, and Mercedes drive their sled onto the thin ice of the river, fall through, and drown. It is London's intention that the reader sees them as unfit to survive since they refused to adapt to their environment, and thereby deserving of their fate.

Critical Level (page 74)
1. John Thornton is the ideal man who has adapted to the wilderness and knows how to live off the land. He has not been brutalized by the harsh environment and still has the capacity for love. He is the only link that Buck has with civilization. It is Buck's love for John that prevents him from answering the call of the wild; therefore, it is necessary to the plot that John die so that this conflict may be resolved. It is up to the students to determine for themselves whether or not John Thornton deserved to die any more or less than Hal, Charles, and Mercedes, in a moral or civilized sense.

2. The plot structure of the novel is episodic; each chapter is a story complete in itself. Some of the characters appear in more than one chapter, but only Buck appears throughout the book. The characters are important only insofar as they affect Buck. After they serve their function they are removed from the plot. The episodic structure is effective in showing Buck's transformation from the sated aristocrat in

ANSWER KEY

Chapter One to the giant timber wolf of Chapter Seven.

3. Some of the themes that are evident in *The Call of the Wild* are:

    (a) the theory of atavism: under certain circumstances a civilized individual will revert to the characteristics and ways of his ancestors
    (b) the will to dominate
    (c) social criticism
    (d) survival of the fittest

Answers to Crossword Puzzle (page 78)

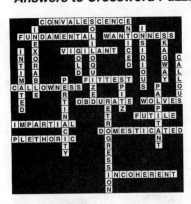

Answers to Test
PART I: VOCABULARY (page 79)

1. plethoric
    (excessively abundant)
2. fundamental
    (basic)
3. impartial
    (unbiased)
4. wantonness
    (malicious, immoral)
5. pertinacity
    (holding firmly to a purpose)
6. soliloquized
    (spoke to oneself)
7. retrogression
    (backward movement or wasteful behavior)
8. callous
    (hardened)
9. intimated
    (hinted)
10. palpitant
    (quivering)
11. domesticated
    (tamed)

12. insidious
    (wily or treacherous)
13. callowness
    (immaturity)
14. convalescence
    (recovery)
15. obdurate
    (stubborn)
16. enticed
    (tempted)
17. incoherent
    (disordered and unconnected)
18. vigilant
    (watchful)
19. futile
    (useless)
20. inexorable
    (unyielding)

PART II: TRUE OR FALSE (page 80)

1. true
2. true
3. false
4. false
5. true
6. false
7. false
8. true
9. false
10. true

PART III: MULTIPLE CHOICE (pages 80-82)

1. A
2. D
3. C
4. C
5. B
6. A
7. D
8. B
9. B
10. B
11. D
12. B
13. A
14. B
15. B

PART IV: ESSAY (page 82)
Answers will vary.

THE RED PONY

by John Steinbeck

SYNOPSIS

Jody knows that something unusual is going on. His father and the ranch hand, Billy Buck, have been in town all day, and Jody can see by the way they're acting that they have special news to tell him.

But they don't tell him. His father just sends him to bed and mentions that they will need him in the morning. Nobody will say what for.

The next morning, neither his father nor Billy will say anything except that Jody should go with them after breakfast. His father sounds cross, and Jody is worried.

Jody goes with the two men to the barn, and what he sees in the stall makes him breathless for a moment. He almost can't believe it. A pony. Jody hears his father telling him to take good care of the pony or it will be sold. Jody's father, as usual, is being strict with his son. But what Jody really hears is his father's way of telling him that the pony is *his.* His own pony!

In part, *The Red Pony* is what the title suggests; the story of a boy and his pony. But only in part. Actually, *The Red Pony* is four separate stories, the first of which concerns the pony, but all four of which concern the boy, Jody, and the experiences which will help shape his view of the way life is.

All four stories, of course, reflect the author, John Steinbeck's, view of the way life is. Basically, it would seem a tragic view. In *The Red Pony,* life by nature is precarious for all creatures—animal and human. Not that there isn't a natural order, but natural patterns of life and death take no account of human hopes and feelings. This is something with which Jody, in *The Red Pony,* must come to terms. Nature might seem to play the role of villain in these four stories. Steinbeck, however, considered nature beyond such labels; neither a villain nor a hero, neither an enemy nor a friend, but simply indifferent. Many of Steinbeck's ideas about nature—about the land and people's relationship to it—he no doubt developed from his own observations.

The setting for *The Red Pony*, and for most of Steinbeck's fiction, is in California, where he was born and grew up. The land and the way of life that Jody knows, Steinbeck himself knew as a boy. Beyond the coastal mountains there is the Pacific, and this, too, was part of Steinbeck's personal boyhood world. Then, in college, he majored in marine biology. What Steinbeck observed and learned during these early years helped to shape his view of nature and of human existence as part of nature.

In *The Red Pony,* if nature is not a villain, there are no human villains, either. Jody's authoritarian father, a man who seems to think it a sign of weakness to show affection, is no hero. But he is hardly a villain, and he loves his son.

There is a hero, apart from Jody himself. He is Billy Buck, the kind of character who appears in many of Steinbeck's stories and novels, usually in a secondary, but important, role. He is Steinbeck's folk hero—the idealized working man, a master of his trade. In Billy's case, he is a top hand with horses. He is also wise and sensitive to other people's feelings. In the first story of *The Red Pony,* called "The Gift," it is Billy who teaches Jody how to take care of and train his gift pony.

Jody puts his weight on the stirrup to get the pony used to it, but he doesn't swing into the saddle yet. His father has told him to hold off trying to ride the pony until Thanksgiving. But before then, it rains for days at a time. Jody keeps the pony in a stall, out of the dampness, except for one day when the rain lets up. Billy assures the boy that more rain is unlikely for awhile, so Jody goes off to school, leaving the pony out in the corral. If it does rain, Billy promises to take the pony in.

It does rain, and Billy doesn't get back in time. The pony is soaked. For once the usually infallible Billy Buck has made a mistake.

Despite rubdowns and nearly constant care by both Jody and Billy, the pony takes cold and becomes sicker and sicker. In addition, twice, high winds blow the barn door open in the night, and the pony gets out to wander in the cold.

As the first story moves rapidly to a climax, Jody faces the first great emotional crisis of his young life.

The second story or episode in *The Red Pony* takes place much later. It opens with Jody wondering about the mountains near his father's ranch. What lies up there? Not many people have ever been to see. Though this story is called "The Great Mountains," it centers not so much on the mountains as on an old man, Gitano, whom Jody first sees coming up the road to the ranch house.

The man, Gitano, says he was born here, in an adobe house that existed before the present ranch. Now, the old man says, he has come back to stay until he dies. Jody's father will have none of this. He doesn't need an old man to work for him—he is only a small rancher. The old man may stay the night, but the next morning, after breakfast, he must leave.

Jody is interested in the old man. Having shown him the bunkhouse where he can sleep, Jody then takes him out to look at the horses. Gitano, Jody learns, was back in the mountains a long time ago, but doesn't remember much about them.

One of the horses is old Easter, 30-years-old. The first horse Jody's father ever owned—a good horse once, but as the old man himself says, "no good anymore." The comparison between the old man and the old horse is obvious. The next morning, Jody and his parents learn from a neighbor that Gitano has taken old Easter and ridden off. They were last seen heading back into the great mountains.

It is a small incident in Jody's life, but it leaves him with a feeling of great sadness and a painful insight into the nature of human existence.

In the third story, called "The Promise," Jody continues his learning experiences. His father gives him the opportunity to have another horse. Jody can get Nellie, the mare, bred, and his father will pay the stud fee if Jody will do extra work on the ranch. When the colt is born, it'll be Jody's. Jody, of course, agrees, although it means a lot of hard work to earn the stud fee, and it'll be nearly a year before Nellie is ready to give birth.

When Jody isn't working or taking special care of Nellie while she is carrying the colt, he daydreams of what the colt will be like as a full-grown horse with Jody riding him. What is more, Billy has promised that Jody will have a good colt—Billy will see to it. And as Jody's father says, "No one knows more than Billy about how to help a mare deliver a colt."

The time comes one morning just before dawn. Billy rouses Jody out of bed and they rush to the barn. But then, Jody has another painful lesson to learn about life and death and the ways of nature. The colt is turned around wrong inside Nellie, and Billy realizes he can't save both the mare and the colt, so he does what he feels he has to do.

The fourth, and final, story is called "The Leader of the People." Its central character is another old man: Jody's grandfather. He really was a leader of the people. A long time ago, he led a wagon train across the plains to the Pacific Coast. It was the big event of his life and he never tires of telling about it. However, Jody's father, and even Billy and Jody's mother, are tired of hearing about it. Only Jody is really interested. He too, someday, would like to be a leader of the people. But "westering," as Jody's grandfather calls it, is finished. The frontier is gone. Everyplace is settled and has been for a long time. Yet, the reader is left to wonder, might there still be something to take its place? And might there still be a need for leaders of the people?

Now, read the novel to find out what happens in each of these stories!

BIBLIOGRAPHY

Beach, Joseph Warren, *American Fiction 1920-1940.* New York: Russell and Russell, 1960.

Burke, W.J. and Will D. Howe, *American Authors and Books: 1640 to the Present Day.* Revised by Irving R. Weiss. New York: Crown Publishers, Inc., 1943.

Cowley, Malcolm, *The Literary Situation.* New York: the Viking Press, 1943.

Ethridge, James M. (ed.) *Contemporary Authors,* Vol. 2. Detroit: Gale Research Company, 1963.

Fontenrose, Joseph E., *John Steinbeck.* New York: Barnes & Noble, 1963.

French, Warren, *John Steinbeck.* New Haven, Connecticut: College & University Press, 1961.

Geismar, Maxwell, *Writers in Crisis: American Novel Between Two Wars.* New York: Houghton Mifflin, 1942.

Hart, James David, *The Oxford Companion to American Literature.* Fourth edition. New York: Oxford University Press, 1965.

Heiney Donald, *Recent American Literature,* Vol. 4. Woodbury, New York: Barron's Educational Series, Inc., 1958.

Hoffman, Frederick J., *The Modern Novel in America: 1900-1950.* Chicago: Henry Regnery Company, 1951.

Hoffman, Hester R., *Reader's Adviser and Bookman's Manual.* New York: R.R. Bowker, 1964.

James, Mertice M. and Dorothy Brown, *Book Review Digest: Forty-first annual accumulation.* New York: H.W. Wilson Co., 1946.

Jones, Howard Mumford and Richard M. Ludwig, *Guide to American Fiction and Its Backgrounds Since 1890.* Cambridge, Massachusetts: Harvard University Press, 1964.

Kunitz, Stanley J. (ed.), *Twentieth Century Authors,* First Supplement. New York: H.W. Wilson Company, 1955.

Spiller, Robert E. and others, *Literary History of the United States* (History), Third edition, New York: MacMillan Company, 1963.

Steinbeck, John, *The Portable Steinbeck.* Selected by Pascal Covici, enlarged edition. New York: Viking Press, 1946.

Stuckey, William J., *The Pulitzer Prize Novels: A Critical Backward Look.* Norman University of Oklahoma Press, 1966.

Tedlock, E.W. Jr., and C.B. Wicker (ed.), *Steinbeck and His Critics: A Record of Twenty-five Years, a collection of comprehensive and significant essays.* Albuquerque, University of New Mexico Press, 1957.

JOHN STEINBECK

Born in Salinas, California, in 1902, John Steinbeck based many of his stories on this area in northern California. He worked in a variety of occupations, such as painter, hod-carrier, ranch hand, and fruit-picker, before eventually becoming a reporter.

Steinbeck was the recipient of both the Nobel prize for literature in 1962 and the Pulitzer prize in 1940 for his epic novel *The Grapes of Wrath*. He is probably most famous for *The Grapes of Wrath*, a novel about the migration of "Okies" to California during the Great Depression of the 1930's. Most of Steinbeck's novels are based on the themes of poverty, hard luck, and tragedy.

Steinbeck's first successful novel was *Of Mice and Men*, which was published in 1937. It is the story of two drifters, one of whom is somewhat retarded, who find work on a California ranch and dream of a time when they will have a place of their own. But, as in most Steinbeck novels, their dreams are interrupted by tragedy. The story was later made into a play and a motion picture.

His other books include *Tortilla Flat* (1935), *In Dubious Battle* (1936), *The Red Pony* (1937), *The Moon is Down* (1942), *Cannery Row* (1944), *The Pearl* (1945), *East of Eden* (1952), *Sweet Thursday* (1954), *The Short Reign of Pippin IV* (1957), *The Winter of Our Discontent* (1961), and *Travels with Charley* (1962). In 1943 Steinbeck began work as a European correspondent for the *New York Herald Tribune*, and in 1948 he published *Russian Journal*, which describes a trip through Russia.

Steinbeck did not live a particularly extraordinary life. He enjoyed high school and participated in sports, but although he attended Stanford University sporadically from 1919 to 1925, he never completed a degree. In order to learn about and understand the experiences of migrant workers in the 1930's, he went to Oklahoma and joined a group of farmers who were leaving for California. He lived with them for two years, and this background became the basis for *The Grapes of Wrath,* which is generally considered to be his best work.

John Steinbeck died of a heart attack in 1969. His ashes are buried in Salinas, California.

Bibliography
Contemporary Authors, New Revision Series, Vol. 35. Detroit: Gale Research Co., 1992

Date _____ Name _____

AUTHOR PROFILE

Some of the answers to the following questions may be found in the biography on the preceding page. For other information, check your library.

AUTHOR'S NAME :   *John Steinbeck*

1. What has this author written?_____

_____

2. Date of birth _____ Date of death _____

3. What does/did this author look like? _____

_____

_____

4. Where did this author grow up?_____

5. Did this author have any particular difficulties in his life? What were they?

_____

_____

6. What kinds of things does/did this author like to write about most?_____

_____

7. What kind of education does/did this author have?_____

8. What kinds of jobs did this author hold?_____

9. What did you find to be particularly interesting when reading about this author's life?

_____

_____

10. If you could talk to this author in person, what would you like to ask him?

_____

Date _____ Name _____

(WORD STUDY)

Define the underlined words:

1. In *The Red Pony*, life by nature is <u>precarious</u> for all creatures—animal and human.

_____

2. Many of Steinbeck's ideas about nature he no doubt developed from his own <u>observations</u>.

_____

3. Jody's <u>authoritarian</u> father, a man who seems to think it a sign of weakness to show affection, <u>is no hero</u>.

_____

4. He is Steinbeck's folk hero; the <u>idealized</u> working man, a master of his trade.

_____

5. Jody puts his weight on the <u>stirrup</u> to get the pony used to it, but he doesn't swing into the saddle yet.

_____

6. Billy assures the boy that more rain is unlikely for awhile, so Jody goes off to school, leaving the pony out in the <u>corral</u>.

_____

7. For once the usually <u>infallible</u> Billy Buck has made a mistake.

_____

8. The man, Gitano, says he was born here, in an <u>adobe</u> house that existed before the present ranch.

_____

9. Billy <u>rouses</u> Jody out of bed and they rush to the barn.

_____

10. The <u>frontier</u> is gone. Everyplace is settled and has been for a long time.

_____

Date _____ Name _____

(ANTICIPATION GUIDE)

for the novel *The Red Pony*

The numbered questions can be answered from reading the synopsis for the novel. Express your own thoughts when answering the questions that are marked with a ⟹.

1. What is the setting for the novel? _____

⟹ Do you think it is important that Steinbeck knew this location so well? Why or why not?

_____

_____

2. What kind of man is Jody's father? _____

_____

⟹ Do you think the relationship between father and son will change during the course of the novel? Explain.

_____

_____

3. Who does Jody meet in the story called "The Great Mountains"? _____

_____

⟹ How do you think this person might be significant to Jody's life? _____

_____

4. How does Jody get the opportunity to get another horse? _____

_____

⟹ Which do you think Billy will save—the mare or the colt? _____

_____

5. Who is the central character in "The Leader of the People"? _____

_____

⟹ Do you think there are any frontiers left in the world? List them. _____

_____

Date _____ Name _____

THE RED PONY
Word Search

Using the clues below, find the answers hidden in the puzzle and circle them. They may be printed horizontally, vertically, diagonally, or backward. All of the words are associated with the novel in some way.

```
W E F T A V D Z U E L N E V U C T N K Q
P C A O Y W P G D U A E J G Y D O J K K
N A U D U I H L N D B D I H H R G P K O
G L I E P R K A G J H Z O H P E H L B P
U I T C H Y D U Z T N C Y B W I Y P J W
E F I O H W J W J E G J R G E T Z D B Q
Q O F R S I S O U M K N G M M N F E S X
A R V R W W R N H P W V L W D O E Z U H
U N H A B R J S O N Q P H O X R I I O G
T I K L D N K O E I S U V F V F I L I R
H A F B P Y D B K S T T H M B B U A R R
O I E B W B S Q P P U A E R W U D E A G
R Y C I X L K C U R P O V I Q A B D C K
I Y J L B U W S R G P V R R N V J I E P
T G T L P N R Y R E D F W W E B E K R U
A K L Y L D P I I G F X K C R S E N P O
R T A B Z Z J D T X Z R Z J O N B C V T
I T J U R H F S S E A L W W Q M H O K D
A Z I C E O N J Z M O U N T A I N S M Q
N J U K K T A H U A E L B I L L A F N I
```

1. sun-dried brick
2. state where novel takes place
3. a region next to unexplored territory
4. the young boy in the novel
5. things that are noticed
6. a footrest on a saddle
7. enforces obedience
8. an enclosure for animals
9. perfect
10. author of *The Red Pony* (two words)
11. risky
12. the ranch hand (two words)
13. number of stories in the novel
14. incapable of error
15. where Gitano is last seen heading
16. wakes up

Date _____ Name _____

QUESTIONS FOR STUDY AND DISCUSSION

for the novel *The Red Pony*

Literal Level

1. What are the mistakes that Billy Buck makes which result in the sickness and death of Gabilan?

_____

_____

_____

_____

2. Why did Gitano come to the Tiflin Ranch?

_____

_____

_____

_____

3. What decision is Billy Buck forced to make when Nellie is trying to give birth to her colt?

_____

_____

_____

4. Why is Carl annoyed to find out that Grandfather is coming for a visit?

_____

_____

_____

_____

Date _____ Name _____

QUESTIONS FOR STUDY AND DISCUSSION

for the novel *The Red Pony*

Interpretive Level

1. Why does Jody hate buzzards?

_____

_____

_____

_____

2. Why is Gitano considered a pathetic figure?

_____

_____

_____

_____

3. Grandfather compares a mouse hunt to when the troops were hunting Indians. How are these two events similar?

_____

_____

_____

_____

Date _____ Name _____

QUESTIONS FOR STUDY AND DISCUSSION

for the novel *The Red Pony*

Critical Level

1. Do you think Jody is closer to his father or to Billy Buck? Explain.

_____

_____

_____

_____

_____

2. What is the quality of leadership that is emphasized in "The Leader of the People"? What characters in the novel possess this quality? What modern leaders can you name who possess this quality?

_____

_____

_____

_____

_____

(ACTIVITIES)

for the novel *The Red Pony*

♣ Debate the following question:

> • Should parents be stern disciplinarians?

♣ Read Steinbeck's *Of Mice and Men* and *The Pearl.* Compare the characters of Slim and Kino with Billy Buck of *The Red Pony.*

♣ Research the Salinas Valley and Monterey, California areas. Report on the history, development, and people of the region. Prepare a bulletin board display depicting life in these areas.

♣ Draw a map of Southern California and Baja, California. Indicate on the map the approximate location of the Tiflin Ranch. If you are familiar with other novels or stories by John Steinbeck set in this general area, label the specific locations with novel or story titles.

♣ Draw scenes from *The Red Pony.* Post them on the walls of the classroom.

♣ Essay or discussion topics:

> • What responsibilities should parents assign their children?
> • Is death necessary to life?
> • How important is the past?
> • How important are material possessions?
> • What is man's relationship to nature?

♣ Dramatize selected passages from the novel for the rest of the class.

Date _____ Name _____

VOCABULARY

from the novel *The Red Pony*

* *

Define the underlined word in each sentence.

1. Billy's eyes were a <u>contemplative</u>, watery gray.

_____

2. Billy had no right to be <u>fallible</u>, and he knew it.

_____

3. Doubletree Mutt sat still, as though he knew some <u>solemn</u> thing was happening.

_____

4. Jody was ashamed because of older people's <u>potential</u> opinion.

_____

5. The skin of Gitano's face had shrunk back against the skull until it defined bone, not flesh, and made the nose and chin seem sharp and <u>fragile</u>.

_____

6. "I was born here," Gitano said in gentle <u>rebuke</u>.

_____

7. Jody went to his work with <u>unprecedented</u> seriousness.

_____

8. The bay mare Nellie quickly grew <u>complacent</u>.

_____

9. The black cypress tree by the bunkhouse was as <u>repulsive</u> as the water-tub was dear.

_____

10. The dogs leaped aside and whined with <u>apprehension</u>.

_____

VOCABULARY

from the novel *The Red Pony*

* *

Define the underlined word in each sentence.

11. Carl Tiflin was <u>jovial</u> this morning.

_____

12. Mrs. Tiflin's eyes were <u>brooding</u> and kind.

_____

13. For the first time that afternoon, Jody was <u>intent</u>.

_____

14. The very <u>imperturbability</u> of the great mountains was a threat.

_____

15. Gitano's whole body had sagged into a timeless <u>repose</u>.

_____

16. Behind Jody there was a <u>phantom</u> army with great flags and swords.

_____

17. The five dollars his father had advanced reduced Jody to <u>peonage</u> for the whole late spring and summer.

_____

18. Billy knew he had not been <u>infallible</u>.

_____

19. But Jody was filled with terror and <u>desolation</u>.

_____

20. A race of giants had lived then, fearless men, men of <u>staunchness</u> unknown in this day.

_____

Date _____ Name _____

THE RED PONY
CROSSWORD PUZZLE

Use what you have learned from the novel to complete the puzzle. Many of the words are taken from the vocabulary study.

ACROSS

1. self-satisfied
8. Jody's ideal man (two words)
9. arousing disgust
10. delicate
14. tree that symbolizes pain and death
17. contemplative
20. rest
21. concentrated
23. not perfect
24. novel
25. extreme calm

DOWN

2. thoughtful
3. the red pony
4. serious
5. birds that feed on dead animals
6. grief
7. in good humor
11. ghost
12. anxiety
13. sharp criticism
15. strong loyalty
16. old paisano
18. serfdom
19. perfect
22. existing as a possibility

99

Date _____ Name _____

PART I: VOCABULARY (20 points)
Write the definition of the word in the space next to it.

1. brooding _____

2. potential _____

3. staunchness _____

4. repose _____

5. contemplative _____

6. rebuke _____

7. intent _____

8. jovial _____

9. repulsive _____

10. apprehension _____

11. imperturbability _____

12. fallible _____

13. complacent _____

14. desolation _____

15. phantom _____

16. unprecedented _____

17. solemn _____

18. infallible _____

19. fragile _____

20. peonage _____

PART II: TRUE OR FALSE (10 points)

In the space provided write *true* if the statement is completely true, or write *false* if any part of the statement is false.

_____ 1. To Carl Tiflin, showing emotion is a sign of weakness.

_____ 2. Jody blames the buzzards for the death of his pony.

_____ 3. Jody resents having to work all summer to pay off Nellie's stud fee.

_____ 4. Billy Buck kills Nellie in order to keep his promise to Jody.

_____ 5. Jody invites his grandfather to join him in a mouse hunt.

_____ 6. Carl Tiflin believes that children and animals should be coddled.

_____ 7. Billy proves his irresponsibility by allowing Gabilan to stand in the corral during a cold rain.

_____ 8. Gitano steals old Easter and rides off toward the great mountains.

_____ 9. In Part IV of *The Red Pony,* the character who best demonstrates the qualities of a leader of the people is Carl Tiflin.

_____ 10. Grandfather compares the people who made up the westward movement to a big crawling beast.

PART III: MULTIPLE CHOICE (30 points)

Decide which is the best response for each of the following sentences. Write the letter of your choice in the space provided.

_____ 1. Jody hates buzzards, but he is not allowed to hurt them because they:
    (a) are protected by law
    (b) eat carrion
    (c) are too dangerous to molest
    (d) control such pests as rabbits and mice

_____ 2. The major reason Gabilan dies is because:
    (a) Jody was careless in leaving Gabilan in the corral
    (b) Billy Buck failed to put Gabilan in the barn
    (c) Carl Tiflin doesn't take care of the animals
    (d) no one person or thing

_____ 3. Gitano steals Easter because:
    (a) the horse is old and useless, like him
    (b) he is angered by Carl's lack of sympathy
    (c) the horse belonged to him before Carl got it
    (d) he is a thief

_____ 4. "The Promise," which is the title of Part III in *The Red Pony*, refers to:
    (a) Carl's promise to give Jody a second colt
    (b) Jody's promise to take care of Nellie until she throws her colt
    (c) Billy's promise not to let anything happen to the colt
    (d) Carl and Billy's promise to help Jody raise the colt

_____ 5. Jody's decision not to have a mouse hunt:
    (a) symbolizes his rejection of evil
    (b) demonstrates his love of nature
    (c) symbolizes his growing maturity
    (d) demonstrates his hatred of violence

_____ 6. Billy criticizes Carl for:
    (a) failing to understand how Jody feels about the buzzards
    (b) refusing to let Gitano stay on the ranch
    (c) forcing Jody to pay for Nellie's stud fee
    (d) not paying him enough wages

_____ 7. The man who serves as Jody's ideal through most of the novel is:
    (a) Carl
    (b) Gitano
    (c) Grandfather
    (d) Billy Buck

_____ 8. In "The Gift," Billy Buck feels bad about all except one of the following:
    (a) being mistaken about the weather
    (b) failing to put Gabilan in his stall
    (c) not being infallible in Jody's eyes
    (d) cutting a hole in Gabilan's throat

_____ 9. The reason Carl doesn't want Gitano to stay on the ranch is because:
    (a) Gitano is old and useless
    (b) Carl cannot afford to feed another person
    (c) Gitano is a thief
    (d) Carl does not like paisanos

_____ 10. Carl gives Jody a second chance to raise a colt with the understanding that Jody will:
    (a) do all of the chores on the ranch
    (b) take care of Nellie until she throws her colt
    (c) not be careless as he was with Gabilan
    (d) learn all he can about horses from Billy Buck

_____ 11. Jody hopes that Nellie's colt will be a:
    (a) black stallion
    (b) bay mare like Nellie
    (c) red pony like Gabilan
    (d) gentle gelding

_____ 12. Grandfather compares the mouse hunt with:
    (a) a game he played as a child
    (b) wrestling
    (c) killing Indians
    (d) slaughtering pigs

_____ 13. Grandfather is sad and depressed because he thinks that:
    (a) the past is dead and gone
    (b) he is dying
    (c) Jody is irresponsible
    (d) he is no longer a leader of the people

_____ 14. The cypress tree symbolizes:
    (a) sanity and health
    (b) pain and death
    (c) maturity and wisdom
    (d) violence and evil

_____ 15. The wooden tub symbolizes:
    (a) sanity and health
    (b) pain and death
    (c) maturity and wisdom
    (d) violence and evil

PART IV: ESSAY (40 points)

Answer <u>two</u> of the following essay questions.

1. Explain how Jody is influenced by each of the major characters in *The Red Pony*.

2. Explain how each of the four parts of the novel develops the relationship between life and death.

3. How is Jody different or the same at the end of the novel from the way he was at the beginning?

4. Compare Gitano and Grandfather, and describe the influence that each of them has on Jody.

ANSWER KEY

Answers to Word Study (page 90)

1. precarious: risky
2. observations: things that are noticed
3. authoritarian: enforces obedience
4. idealized: perfect
5. stirrup: a footrest on a saddle
6. corral: an enclosure for animals
7. infallible: incapable of error
8. adobe: sun-dried brick
9. rouses: wakes up
10. frontier: a region next to unexplored territory

Answers to Anticipation Guide (page 91)

1. California
2. an authoritarian man who thinks it a sign of weakness to show affection
3. Gitano
4. he can get Nellie bred and his father will pay the stud fee if Jody will do extra work on the ranch
5. Jody's grandfather

Answers to Word Search (page 92)

1. ADOBE
2. CALIFORNIA
3. FRONTIER
4. JODY
5. OBSERVATIONS
6. STIRRUP
7. AUTHORITARIAN
8. CORRAL
9. IDEALIZED
10. JOHN STEINBECK
11. PRECARIOUS
12. BILLY BUCK
13. FOUR
14. INFALLIBLE
15. MOUNTAINS
16. ROUSES

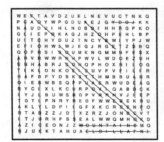

Answers to Questions for Study and Discussion

Literal Level (page 93)

1. He predicted it wouldn't rain; he neglected to put the pony in the barn.
2. To die in the place where he was born.
3. He has to kill Nellie in order to save the colt.
4. He's tired of hearing Grandfather's stories over and over again.

Interpretive Level (page 94)

1. Steinbeck does not tell us specifically why Jody hates buzzards, but we can speculate on the reasons

why most of us are repelled by them: they are ugly; they follow a dying creature; they live off the dead; they eat rotting flesh.

2. He is useless; he is too old to work; all he can do is wait to die.

3. The mice are helpless and are only killed for amusement. Grandfather is saying that the Indians were just as helpless and were slaughtered just as needlessly.

Critical Level (page 95)

1. Steinbeck portrays Carl as stern and authoritarian, unable to express affection. Billy, on the other hand, is more sensitive and compassionate. It is natural that Jody would feel closer to Billy.

2. The quality of leadership that is evident is one's sensitivity to the force that compels an entire people to seek their destiny. Jody is the only character in the novel who understands what his grandfather knows. Students might discuss John Kennedy, Winston Churchill, and Martin Luther King, Jr., as examples of modern leaders who were aware of the drives and hungers of people.

Answers to Crossword Puzzle (page 99)

Answers to Test

PART I: VOCABULARY (page 100)

1. brooding
   (contemplative)
2. potential
   (existing as a possibility)
3. staunchness
   (strong loyalty)
4. repose
   (rest)
5. contemplative
   (thoughtful)

ANSWER KEY

6. rebuke
   (sharp criticism)
7. intent
   (concentrated)
8. jovial
   (in good humor)
9. repulsive
   (arousing disgust)
10. apprehension
    (anxiety)
11. imperturbability
    (extreme calm)
12. fallible
    (not perfect)
13. complacent
    (self-satisfied)
14. desolation
    (grief)
15. phantom
    (ghost)
16. unprecedented
    (novel)
17. solemn
    (serious)
18. infallible
    (perfect)
19. fragile
    (delicate)
20. peonage
    (serfdom)

PART II: TRUE OR FALSE (page 101)
1. true
2. false
3. false
4. true
5. true
6. false
7. false
8. true
9. false
10. true

PART III: MULTIPLE CHOICE (pages 101-103)
1. B
2. D
3. A
4. C
5. C
6. A
7. D
8. D
9. B
10. B
11. A
12. C
13. A
14. B
15. A

PART IV: ESSAY (page 103)
Answers will vary.

Date _____ Name _____

IN MY OPINION . . .

Title of Novel _____

Completely describe your favorite scene **OR** your favorite character from the novel.

_____

_____

_____

_____

_____

_____

_____

_____

_____

_____

_____

_____

_____

_____

_____

Date _____ Name _____

PLOTTING THE PLOT

Title of novel _____

On the lines below, list the major events of the story in the order in which they occur. Then, in the box next to each line, rate each event on a scale of 1 to 10, with 10 being the most important.

☐ _____   ☐ _____

☐ _____   ☐ _____

☐ _____   ☐ _____

☐ _____   ☐ _____

☐ _____   ☐ _____

☐ _____   ☐ _____

After you have rated each event according to its significance to the story, plot each event on the graph. Write the events, in the order that they occur, in the spaces along the bottom of the graph starting on the left side. Then, for each event, put a dot on the graph above the event and across from the number on the left side of the graph which corresponds to your rating of that event.

When you have plotted all the events, draw a line connecting all the dots across the graph.

When you have completed the graph, answer the following questions:

1. Which event did you rate as most important? Why? _____

_____

2. Which event do you feel represents the conflict in the story? _____

_____

3. Which event represents the resolution of the conflict? _____

_____

Constructed by _____

PLOTTING THE PLOT ◆ Title of Novel _____

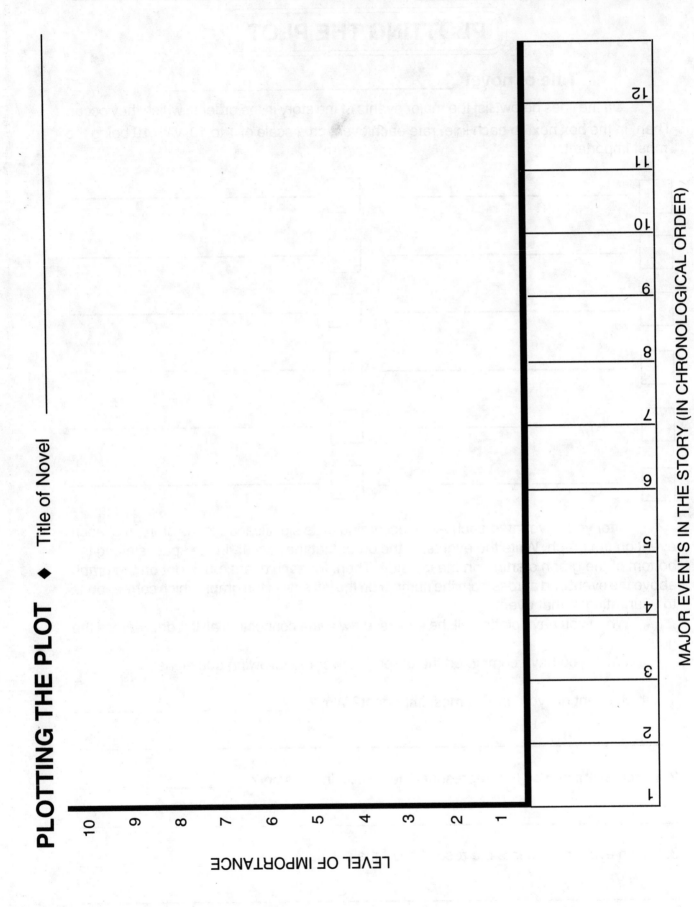

LEVEL OF IMPORTANCE

10 9 8 7 6 5 4 3 2 1

MAJOR EVENTS IN THE STORY (IN CHRONOLOGICAL ORDER)

1 2 3 4 5 6 7 8 9 10 11 12